TOON ART

THE GRAPHIC ART OF DIGITAL CARTOONING

BY STEVEN WITHROW

ILEX

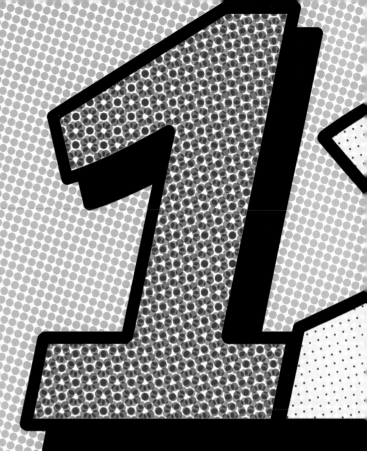

First published in the United Kingdom in 2003 by
ILEX
The Old Candlemakers
West Street
Lewes
East Sussex BN7 2NZ
www.ilex-press.com.

Copyright © 2003 by The Ilex Press Limited

This book was conceived by
ILEX
Cambridge
England

Publisher: Alastair Campbell
Executive Publisher: Sophie Collins
Creative Director: Peter Bridgewater
Editorial Director: Steve Luck
Design Manager: Tony Seddon
Editor: Stuart Andrews
Designer: Jonathan Raimes
Development Art Director: Graham Davis

British Library Cataloguing-in-Publication Data
A catalogue record for this book is available from the British Library

ISBN 1-904705-01-4

Printed and bound in China

TOON ART

contents

Introduction

We see cartoons everywhere – hoardings, newspapers, magazines, books, CD covers, arcade games, product packaging, movie and TV screens and now computer monitors. Pictorial icons, perhaps the simplest kind of cartoon, are as ubiquitous as the written word, and when combined like parts of speech in a visual language, cartoon images hold as much expressive energy as any other communication tool. With so many cartoons around, it follows that we live in a world full of working cartoonists, paid and unpaid, blotting their dreams and thoughts on whatever medium appeals most at the moment – be it paper, plaster or pixelated plastic.

This book asks and attempts to answer the question: How has digital technology altered the way cartoons are created and presented? This alone is a massive, far-reaching subject, and entire books have been and could be written about each of its many facets, including the history, key players, hardware and software applications, economic and cultural impacts, worldwide expansion and future potential. I have tried to cut a wide swathe in my research, but, in the end, this book is only a glimpse at what digital cartooning is and might still be.

The most recognisable (not to mention lucrative) examples of cartoon art, those which make it a global enterprise, are certainly the products of large corporations. It's no secret that the more money one can invest in a project, the greater the possible return on the investment. This logic has encouraged the majority of professional cartoonists throughout the twentieth century to join studios (Walt Disney's 'House of Mouse' being the most famous example), publishing houses and syndicates to find funding for their work and to share resources, brand identity and group status. Printing, distribution and marketing, along with cinema and television placement, remain overwhelmingly expensive, and so corporations have structured their respective industries to suit their own needs, often to the detriment of the independent creator. Still, many solo

cartoonists have persevered against the 'strength in numbers' model, but few have thrived, and thousands have dropped out of the business entirely.

Now, in the twenty-first century, the computer offers the cartoonist new possibilities that might never level the playing field but are already rewriting some of the basic rules of play. The new accessibility and affordability of computer hardware and graphics software have quickly turned yesterday's assembly-line animation and comics factories into today's streamlined, wired-up home studios.

I have centred this book on the new generation of independent digital cartoonists around the world who are attempting (to varying degrees) to go it alone without corporate sponsorship and, even more importantly, to retain ownership of their creations and control of their creative visions. I hope to show what one person or a small group of creators can now accomplish using digital production and delivery tools, especially the Internet, which gives the cartoonist the chance to share with an audience a digitally produced cartoon in interactive digital form. Cartoons can travel at light speed from a cartoonist's computer to the computers of millions of viewers, and those viewers can give feedback and – coming soon to a Web site near you – payment for the work within seconds. Now, if only everyone could download cartoons so quickly!

This book is divided into four parts, following cartooning's historical path from the past to the future. Part One introduces basic definitions of cartooning, comics and animation and then presents a timeline of the history of cartooning. Part Two delves into the creative process as well as the common tools and techniques that make digital cartoons possible. Part Three is a showcase featuring many of today's most innovative comics artists and animators, and Part Four takes a quick look at what tomorrow might have in store for the digital cartoonist. Finally, the book ends with some useful references to help you to investigate digital cartooning on your own.

There are worlds to be drawn, and a world to reach with our drawings. Let us begin.

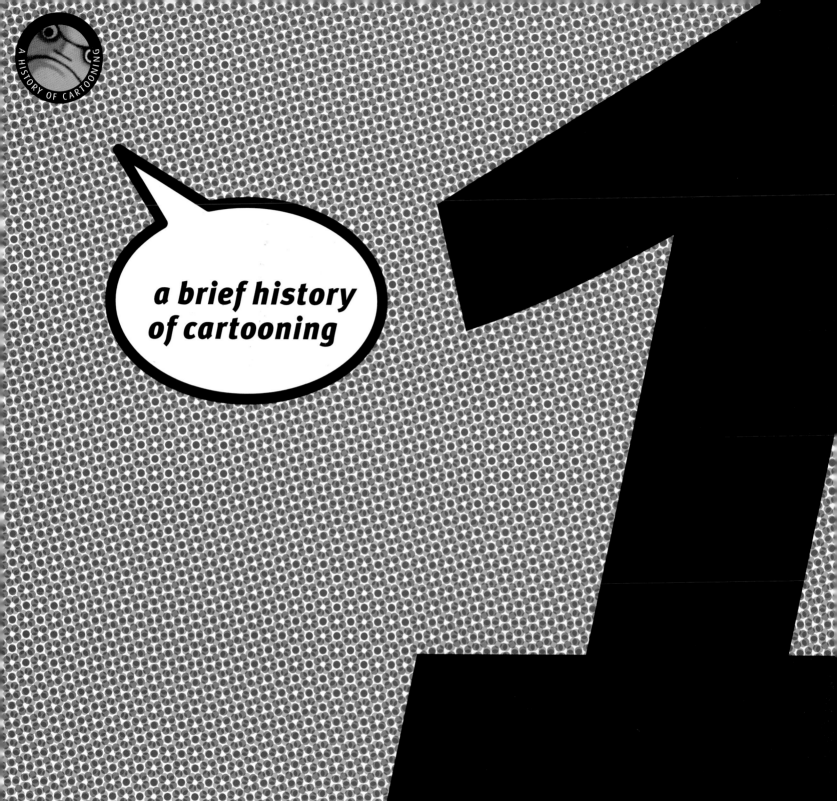

a brief history
of cartooning

9

definitions and divisions

What Is Cartooning?

In his book Understanding Comics (1993), Scott McCloud defines cartooning as 'a form of amplification through simplification'. He goes on to explain, 'When we abstract an image through cartooning, we're not so much eliminating details as we are focusing on specific details. By stripping down an image to its essential "meaning", an artist can amplify that meaning in a way that realistic art can't.'

What are Comics?

Expanding on Will Eisner's term 'sequential art', Scott McCloud defines comics as 'juxtaposed pictorial and other images in deliberate sequence, intended to convey information and/or to produce an aesthetic response in the viewer'. In *Reinventing Comics* (2000), he introduces the term 'temporal map' as a fitting metaphor for the process of placing one image after another to show the passage of time that is central to comics. You may notice that McCloud's definition is not dependent on the content or style of the work, nor is it limited by the technology or the various methods used to create the work.

Above right: *Critics and cartoonists worldwide have hailed Scott McCloud's* Understanding Comics *and* Reinventing Comics *as two of the most important books on the evolution of the comics form.*

What Is Animation?

As McCloud did for comics, master animator and director Gene Deitch sought to propose a technical definition for animation 'without limiting it to a specific technology, that might become obsolete; to try to come up with a bedrock basic statement of stop-motion animation's technical essence'. In his book *How To Succeed in Animation (Don't Let a Little Thing Like Failure Stop You!)* (http://genedeitch.awn.com), Deitch defines frame-by-frame, cinematic animation: 'The recording of individually created phases of imagined action in such as way as to achieve the illusion of motion when shown at a constant, predetermined rate, exceeding that of human persistence of vision.' He points out that 'animation, as with music, is an art form that exists in the dimension of time. It must have uninterrupted movement through time to exist.'

Images by Anzovin Studio

The origins of cartooning may be traced back more than 35,000 years to the cave drawings discovered in recent times at such sites as Lascaux, Altamira and Vallon Pont d'Arc. Today's animations and comics have been linked to a pictorial narrative tradition that spans many cultures and includes works as disparate as The Codex Nuttall of ancient Mexico, medieval Europe's Bayeux Tapestry and Bishop Toba's chojugiga or 'Animal Scrolls' from 12th-century Japan. My choice of starting point for the modern period of cartooning is highly subjective, as is my selection of events, and alternative timelines are equally valid.

Japanese woodblock-print artist Hokusai coins the term 'manga' ('whimsical sketches').

Dominique Seraphin begins presenting *ombres chinoises* or 'shadow theatre' to French audiences.

Punch, a satirical magazine, debuts in England.

The 'Wheel of Life', or zoetrope, a spinning cylinder that gives the appearance of an object in motion, appears in America.

toon timeline

| 1436 | 1640 | 1731 | 1772 | 1814 | 1824 | 1841 | mid 1800s | 1867 | 1877 |

how it all began

Johann Gutenberg invents the printing press in Germany.

William Hogarth publishes *A Harlot's Progress*, a six-plate picture-story.

Frenchman Emile Reynaud introduces the praxinoscope, a device that displayed short sequences of action on a strip of transparent 'Crystaloid'.

An Italian, Athanasius Kircher, introduces the Magic Lantern, which projects images onto a wall or other surface. This remains a popular entertainment form until the Victorian Period.

Peter Mark Roget publishes *Persistence of Vision with Regard to Moving Objects*.

Swiss artist Rodolphe Töpffer begins cartooning, using panel borders and word-and-picture combinations. Other innovators are Germany's Wilhelm Busch, France's Georges ('Christophe') Colomb and Brazil's Angelo Agostini.

Edward Muybridge publishes *The Human Figure in Motion*, still in use today as a reference book for animators.

George Herriman introduces Krazy Kat in his comic strip *The Dingbat Family*.

Comic Monthly magazine reprints newspaper comic strips. The next year, Walt Disney combines live action with animation in *Alice's Wonderland*.

Walt Disney's *Oswald the Lucky Rabbit* cartoon series debuts.

Muybridge adapts Reynaud's praxinoscope to create his zoopraxinoscope.

James Stuart Blackton and Thomas Edison release *The Humorous Phases of Funny Faces*. This is generally considered to be the first animated film.

Winsor McCay releases first dramatic animation, *The Sinking of the Lusitania*.

1879 1896 1901 1905 1906 1908 1910 1914 1918 1919 1922 1926 1927 1928

Winsor McCay's *Little Nemo in Slumberland* appears in *The New York Herald*.

Winsor McCay shows *Gertie the Dinosaur* to Vaudeville audiences. That same year, J R Bray and Earl Hurd apply for animation cel patents.

Lotte Reiniger produces her hour-long, silhouette-style animated film, *Prince Achmed*, in Germany.

Emile Cohl releases animated *Fantasmagorie* in France. A year later, Rose O'Neill sparks a merchandising frenzy in America with her 'Kewpie' characters.

Otto Messmer's Felix the Cat, the most popular cartoon character of the 1920s, appears in *Feline Follies*. Also, Max Fleischer releases the *Out of the Inkwell* cartoons starring Koko the Klown.

Richard Fenton Outcault publishes *The Yellow Kid* comic strip in *The New York World*. Many consider this to be the start of the comics form, but, as this timeline shows, comics have a much longer history.

Walt Disney and Ub Iwerks create the first three Mickey Mouse cartoons: *Plane Crazy*, *The Gallopin' Gaucho* and *Steamboat Willie*.

Jerry Siegel and Joe Schuster's Superman arrives in *Action Comics #1*. The next year, Bob Kane and Bill Finger introduce Batman in *Detective Comics #27*. In animation, Bugs Bunny gets his first cartoon role in *Porky's Hare Hunt*.

Disney releases *Dumbo*. Joe Simon and Jack Kirby introduce *Captain America* in *Timely Comics*. Jack Cole's Plastic Man appears in *Police Comics #1*.

Leon Schlesinger sells his cartoon studio to Warner Brothers. *Looney Toons* and *Merry Melodies* begin colour production. Gene Kelly dances with Jerry Mouse (of *Tom & Jerry*) in the MGM film *Anchors Aweigh*.

Disney's first Technicolour cartoon, *Flowers and Trees,* wins the first Academy Award for animation.

Comic-strip audiences are introduced to Alex Raymond's *Flash Gordon* and Milt Caniff's *Terry and the Pirates*. Also, the first monthly comic book, *Famous Funnies #1*, sells for a dime.

Martin Goodman's Timely Comics publishes *Marvel Comics #1* featuring Bill Everett's The Sub-Mariner and Carl Burgos's The Human Torch.

Carl Barks creates Uncle Scrooge for Disney's *Four Color Comics #178*.

Chester Gould's *Dick Tracy* makes his comic-strip debut.

1929	1931	1932	1933	1934	1937	1938	1939	1940	1941	1942	1943	1944	1945	1947

Tarzan, Popeye the Sailor and Buck Rogers appear in comic strips. Also, Disney's first Silly Symphonies cartoon, *The Skeleton Dance,* is released. In Belgium, cartoonist Herge (Georges Remi) begins his *Tintin* comics, a primary influence on European comics and *bande dessinée*.

A song from Walt Disney's *Three Little Pigs* cartoon becomes a national hit in Depression-era America. Also that year, *Funnies on Parade* reprints Sunday comic strips in colour.

Walt Disney introduces the multiplane camera, and *Snow White and the Seven Dwarfs* becomes Disney's first feature-length animated cartoon. In the print world, Charles Addams publishes the first *Addams Family* cartoon in *The New Yorker*, and *Detective Comics #1* debuts.

Walt Disney releases *Fantasia* and *Pinocchio*, Walter Lantz creates *Woody Woodpecker*, and Hanna-Barbera begin *Tom & Jerry* cartoons for MGM. Fawcett Publications introduces *Captain Marvel*, created by C.C. Beck and William Parker. Will Eisner's 'Spirit Section' begins distribution in American newspapers.

Paul Terry's Terrytoons parodies Superman in *The Mouse of Tomorrow* (Mighty Mouse). Disney releases *Bambi*.

Tex Avery directs Droopy and Red Hot Riding Hood cartoons for MGM. Leon Schlesinger produces Private Snafu cartoons for the US Army.

Harry Smith produces animation by drawing directly onto film. Chuck Jones directs Pepe LePew cartoons for Warner Brothers.

Mad Comics, created by Harvey Kurtzman and many other great cartoonists, is published by EC Comics and will go on (becoming *Mad Magazine* in 1955) to be the most popular American humour periodical of all time. Meanwhile, in Japan, Osamu Tezuka's *Tetsuwan Atomu* ('Mighty Atom', later published in English as *Astro Boy*) helps to ignite a hunger for Japanese manga and anime (comics and animation) unparalleled in any

other nation. This will culminate, in the early 1980s, in the publication of more than one billion copies of manga titles each year. Manga has a much wider array of genres than comics do in the US, and manga artists often employ sophisticated graphic storytelling techniques that are sometimes tough for non-Japanese readers to grasp. Cartooning is a central part of Japanese culture, and is now expanding worldwide.

Road Runner and Wile E. Coyote make their cartoon debut in *The Fast and Furry-ous* (directed by Chuck Jones) for Warner Brothers.

EC Comics ceases to publish all comic-book titles.

Jay Ward's *Rocky & Bullwinkle* cartoons premiere on television. Disney releases *Sleeping Beauty*, and UPA releases *1001 Arabian Nights*. In France, Rene Goscinny and Albert Uderzo begin publishing their *Asterix* comics in *Pilote* magazine. Graphic albums and animations of the *Asterix* stories will become hugely popular worldwide.

Disney releases *101 Dalmations.* Croatia's Zagreb Animation Studio wins an Academy Award. Stan Lee and Jack Kirby create *Fantastic Four #1*, ushering in the 'Marvel Age' for comic books. At MIT, Ivan E Sutherland begins work on Sketchpad, a program for interactive computer graphics.

Ken Knowlton and Stan Vanderbeek create *Poem Field* using computer animation techniques at Bell Laboratories.

1949 1950 1952 1954 1955 1956 1957 1958 1959 1960 1961 1962 1963 1964

Disney's *Cinderella* premieres. UPA's adaptation of Dr Seuss's *Gerald McBoing Boing* wins Oscar for best animated film. On the newspaper page, Charles M Schulz begins his 50-year run on *Peanuts*.

Psychologist Frederic Wertham attacks comics as a cause of juvenile delinquency in his book *Seduction of the Innocent*. The US Senate holds hearings on comic books, at which EC publisher William M Gaines testifies. The Comics Magazine Association of America and The Comics Code are established to censor comics of any 'questionable' material before publication.

Art Clokey's stop-motion clay animation, *Gumby & Friends*, appears on television.

John Whitney experiments with analogue computer graphics. Joseph Hanna and William Barbera begin creating animation for television with *Ruff & Reddy*.

Jules Feiffer syndicates his *Feiffer* comic strip.

Primetime television (CBS network) welcomes Hanna-Barbera's *The Flintstones* and *The Bugs Bunny TV Show* from Warner Brothers. Disney uses Xerox Process in animation.

Marvel Comics introduces Spider-Man in *Amazing Fantasy #15*.

Marvel Comics publishes *The Uncanny X-Men #1*. The first comic-book convention is organized in New York City. Warner Brothers closes its animation studio. The first computer-generated film is created by Edward Zajec of Bell Laboratories (USA).

Zap Comix #1, a 24-page underground comic book, is published. The first videotaped movies are introduced for home use. *Speed Racer*, one of the most popular Japanese cartoon exports, is released in the US.

At Xerox Palo Alto, Richard G Shoup creates SuperPaint, an 8-bit digital painting system.

George Lucas releases *Star Wars*, to global acclaim. Canadian cartoonist Dave Sim self-publishes *Cerebus*, inspiring many independent comics artists to 'do it yourself'.

Kevin Eastman and Peter Laird self-publish *Teenage Mutant Ninja Turtles #1*, a runaway success that sparks a brief 'black-and-white explosion' in comics. The first Macintosh computer is sold.

Barry Windsor-Smith illustrates a series based on Robert E Howard's *Conan the Barbarian* pulp stories for Marvel Comics.

Produced by the National Film Board of Canada, Peter Foldes and Rene Jodoin's Oscar-winning *Hunger* is the first computer-generated 2D animation short.

Art Spiegelman's avant-garde *RAW* anthologies feature work from Charles Burns, Drew Friedman and Gary Panter. Quantel (UK) introduces Paintbox, a system that is widely used for digital design in film and television.

'Underground' cartoonist Robert Crumb publishes *Fritz the Cat*. Ralph Bakshi creates an animated version in 1972.

| 1965 | 1966 | 1967 | 1968 | 1970 | 1972 | 1973 | 1974 | 1975 | 1977 | 1978 | 1980 | 1981 | 1982 | 1984 |

Chuck Jones adapts and directs Dr Seuss's *How the Grinch Stole Christmas* for television. Walt Disney dies on December 15.

The Beatles' film, *The Yellow Submarine*, is released. The Special Interest Group on Computer Graphics (SIGGRAPH) is formed.

Disney releases the animated *Robin Hood*. Hanna-Barbera releases an animated adaptation of E B White's *Charlotte's Web*. Ralph Bakshi debuts a semi-autobiographical animated film, *Heavy Traffic*.

French cartoonists Jean Giraud (Moebius), Jean-Pierre Dionnet and Phillip Druillet publish *Metal Hurlant*, a European science-fiction comics anthology. In 1977, it is released in America as *Heavy Metal*. Also in 1975, Phil Seuling begins direct distribution to comics speciality shops.

Ralph Bakshi animates J R R Tolkien's *The Lord of the Rings*. Will Eisner publishes *A Contract with God*, which he calls a 'graphic novel'.

Disney's new generation of animators releases *The Fox and the Hound*.

Ralph Bakshi directs animation sequences for Pink Floyd's *The Wall*, designed by Gerald Scarfe. Don Bluth releases *The Secret of NIMH*. Fantagraphics publishes *Love and Rockets* by Los Bros Hernandez. Disney's *Tron* uses 15 minutes of digital animation.

Comics fans watch in awe as *Watchmen* by Alan Moore and Dave Gibbons, *The Dark Knight Returns* by Frank Miller and *Maus: A Survivor's Tale* by Art Spiegelman (winner of the Pulitzer Prize) all see print. Animation fans see the future with Pixar's *Luxo Jr.* digital short. The Comic Book Legal Defense Fund is founded.

Neil Gaiman and Dave McKean's long-running *Sandman* series debuts from DC Comics. Disney's *The Little Mermaid* premieres. Adobe introduces Photoshop software for Macintosh.

Image Comics is formed. The inflated comic-book speculator market causes a glut of new titles to be published. Ted Turner launches The Cartoon Network for cable TV. Disney releases *Aladdin*. DC Comics begins its 'mature-reader' Vertigo line of comics. Mike Judge brings the *Beavis & Butt-Head* animated series to MTV. Paul Dini and Bruce Timm debut *Batman: The Animated Series* on Fox.

© Disney Enterprises, Inc.

Disney releases *The Lion King.* Mosaic introduces the World Wide Web to desktop computers. DreamWorks SKG launches.

Disney's *Dinosaur* combines digital characters with photographed natural backgrounds. Disney's symphonic *Fantasia* 2000 mixes traditional and digital animation. Innovative CrossGen Comics enters the direct market. Stan Lee Media, an early pioneer of webcomics and online animation, declares bankruptcy as the 'Dotcom Crash' becomes a harsh reality for many Internet businesses. Scott McCloud publishes *Reinventing Comics,* which sends a rallying cry to Web cartoonists worldwide.

Disney/Pixar releases *A Bug's Life.*

Nickelodeon releases *Jimmy Neutron: Boy Genius.*

1986 1988 1989 1990 1991 1992 1993 1994 1995 1998 1999 2000 2001 2002

Matt Groening's *The Simpsons* becomes a primetime TV cartoon on Fox network. Pepe Moreno creates *Batman: Digital Justice* using a Macintosh for DC Comics.

Stephen Spielberg presents the *Animaniacs* cartoon series. Nick Park's *The Wrong Trousers* and Tim Burton's *The Nightmare Before Christmas* take stop-motion animation to a higher level. Scott McCloud publishes *Understanding Comics.*

Hayao Miyazaki's anime *Princess Mononoke* is released in the US. The Disney/Pixar sequel to *Toy Story, Toy Story 2,* is as successful as the original. Warner Brothers The *Iron Giant* is a critical success.

Shrek (DreamWorks SKG) bested *Monsters, Inc.* (Disney/Pixar) for the first Academy Award for feature-length animated film. Disney releases *Treasure Planet,* a digital-age retelling of Robert Louis Stevenson's *Treasure Island.* Genndy Tartovsky's *Powerpuff Girls* and *Samurai Jack* capture a new generation of animation fans on Cartoon Network.

Disney's *Who Framed Roger Rabbit* combines live action and animation expertly. Katsuhiro Otomo's *Akira* manga goes to America courtesy of the Epic line from Marvel Comics.

Disney releases *Beauty and the Beast,* which makes impressive use of digitally designed backgrounds. John Kricfalusi's *Ren & Stimpy* cartoons debut on Nickelodeon. MTV airs its *Liquid Television* animation series.

Disney/Pixar releases *Toy Story,* the first ever feature-length digitally animation.

the creative process

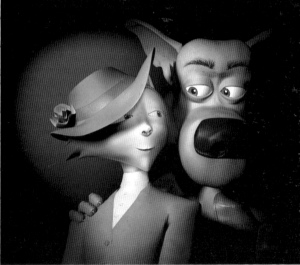

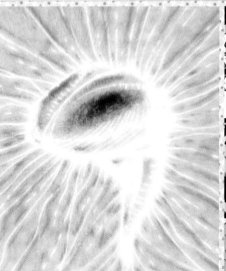

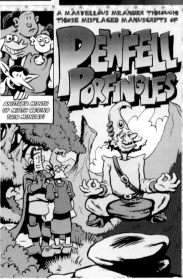

creating digitally

There are as many creative paths as there are cartoonists, but almost every one begins with the urge to communicate an idea, evoke an emotion or tell a story. The methods and materials cartoonists use to fulfil those desires are as innumerable as the layers of the imagination.

With digital tools, complex tasks such as inking and colouring can be handled easily by a single creator.

Environments and designs like this one would be difficult to replicate without the use of digital tools .

Creating digitally affords the cartoonist an 'instant-access' medium and a remarkable array of tools. But where do you start and what choices and challenges will you face? If you choose the digital route, then you'll need a computer, of course – preferably one with a fast Web connection and a scanner. Next you'll need the proper software to format, enhance and for animation, enliven your images and words. What you buy will depend on what you're trying to do: every artist has unique needs and preferences.

While creating digital work may be your goal, you might want to make your first attempts at cartooning using that most reliable of technologies, the blank sheet of paper. The only tool you'll need is a pencil, pen or your drawing implement of choice. There's no software to load and learn, no hardware to repair and update, no broadband connection to purchase and install. It's just you and the wide-open page. So, clear your mind, pick up your pencil and draw.

As your doodles become sketches and your sketches become comics, you might wonder how and where your work fits in the great cartooning continuum. We all judge our work against the creations of others, and most of us seek a historical and cultural context for even our most personal scribblings. There is a competitive spirit in all art, even if the only challenger you have in mind is yourself. The drive to excel, to surpass one's own limitations, is bolstered by a solid education in the principles and practices of art.

Getting a good education does not necessarily mean forking out thousands of pounds in art-school tuition bills and correspondence-course fees. While the 'formal' route has many merits, among them a healthy dose of art theory and history – as well as a close-knit community of fellow creative types – an individual artist, if sufficiently self-motivated, can succeed on his or her own through study and practice.

Left: *Digital images from demian.5's innovative webcomic,* **When I Am King.**

Getting Started

The digital cartoonist often begins with questions of form – namely, what shape and structure should a digital cartoon take? If we return to my initial definitions of cartooning, comics and animation from Chapter One and apply our knowledge of computers, it then becomes apparent that the digital canvas opens up a range of formal possibilities that many print cartoonists might see as unworkable and even ludicrous to attempt on paper. Digital cartooning is such a young and energetic medium that its best days are probably still to come, but take a look at the showcase in Chapter Three for some amazing examples of what is already possible.

While so much opportunity for invention might be liberating, it can also be intimidating for the newcomer. Here are some common forms and formats now in use online (for a selection of common formulas or genres, see Chapter Three):

- ★ Comic strips
- ★ One-shot stories
- ★ Serialized stories
- ★ Long-form stories
- ★ Limited animation
- ★ Full animation
- ★ Screen-by-screen
- ★ Scrolling
- ★ 'Infinite canvas'
- ★ Illustrated prose/verse
- ★ Experimental forms

Trying It Out

Ready to give digital cartooning a try? For the remainder of the chapter, I have enlisted the help of illustrator and designer Patrick Coyle to guide you through nine basic steps in the process of creating a one-page digital comic meant for reading online.

This is where the real fun – and the true work – of digital cartooning begins.

A Nine-Step Creative Process

1	Choosing form, format and formula
2	Creating characters
3	Writing a storyline
4	Sketching backgrounds and composition
5	Drawing characters
6	Colouring
7	Lettering
8	Altering digitally
9	Editing and posting

Choosing Form, Format and Formula

Ninja 'Flying-Heel-to-Eyeball-Kick-Splode' Attack!

Quentin?

The lines that separate form from format and format from formula are tenuous ones. But I think of form as a set of limits or rules that divide one category of art from another. What distinguishes painting from comics, for example, is the addition in comics of a deliberate sequence of images (see Part One for a better definition). Format is the set of methods and materials the creator uses to present an artwork to an audience. Formula is the type or genre of the work that is presented.

For simplicity's sake, Patrick Coyle and I decided to forego the use of animation or other experimental devices such as hyperlinks or sound, keeping our work firmly rooted in the comics form. We chose a conventional format for our comic, the nine-panel grid. Knowing that nine panels are tough to fit on a screen without scrolling, we decided to use the screen-by-screen approach and divide the page into three, three-panel pieces. We then looked at our strengths and interests as creators and opted for a humorous comic that parodied the realistic character drama or 'slice-of-life' comic. I chose the title *Life of Slice* to give our comic a little added panache.

Above: *Ninja comedy in a scrolling vertical format: D. Merlin Goodbrey's short* Dismember.

Left: *A storybook-style page from the illustrated online tale* Catalpa Tears *by Kent Sherrard and Rigel Stuhmiller.*

Once there was a young man, a weaver, who fell deeply in love with a beautiful girl who lived in his village. When she passed, he felt like he had lost his voice or his bones. He spent each night lost in thoughts about her and each day hoping to catch even the shortest glimpse of her.

Now, this beautiful girl was the daughter of the village's richest man, a conniving and deceitful merchant. For forty days and nights the young man wondered how he would get the girl's attention, for he was only a penniless weaver. At last he realized he could only give her what he knew best. So, for seven days he did not sleep. He gathered the leaves of the catalpa trees that grew around his cabin. He wove them into a dazzling dress and left it on the stairs of the girl's house.

Creating Characters

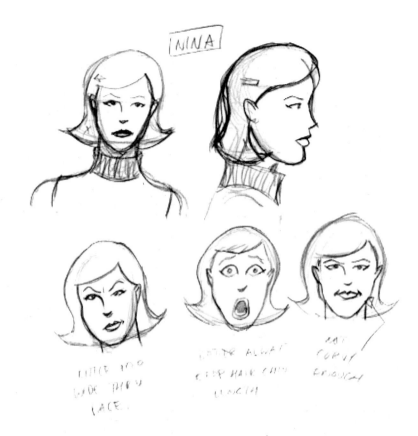

Character is the fundamental element of all narrative. Stories can exist without a definable setting, plot or theme, but it is difficult to imagine a story without a central character, human or otherwise, in some sort of conflict. Therefore, it is the primary job of all cartoonists to populate their stories with at least one character. Creating characters may not always be the first step in the creative process – cartoonists often have story/gag scenarios or 'what-ifs' in mind and craft characters to fit their ideas – but situation and setting are ultimately secondary to the revelation of character through conflict.

While there are many character routes or arcs, here's a simple description of how a character drives a story forwards. The central character (also called the protagonist or hero) has a goal and decides to try to attain it. Conflict appears when someone or something gets in the protagonist's way. This obstacle (also called the antagonist or villain) can be as uncomplicated as a human rival or as complex as the protagonist's own personality. The antagonist also has a goal, and this goal is often in direct opposition to the protagonist's. The story shows which of the two goals – if either – will triumph. The other players in the story (i.e., everyone who interacts with the protagonist/antagonist or inhabits the story's setting) are considered 'minor characters' and serve mainly to help to define the protagonist or antagonist. (See page 26 for more about story structure).

How does all this play out in an actual comic? For *Life of Slice* I envisioned a man, Tom, who has found his relationship with his wife, Nina, to be changing in a way he doesn't like. He is determined to make sense of the change and return the situation to what he sees as 'normal'. Tom decides to speak to Nina about his feelings, and this is where I chose to begin his story, following the couple through a single short scene.

Now, one might assume that Nina is automatically the antagonist of the story, with Tom as the protagonist, since I have introduced no other characters. However, I decided instead to make Tom his own sparring partner, with Nina as simply a mildly impatient observer of her husband grappling with his own insecurities. Tom is, in effect, both protagonist and antagonist.

I set the story in contemporary America, in a modest, middle-class apartment, as this is a milieu both the artist and I know well. I could have chosen, however, to set Tom's story in another time, on another planet, or in the sixth dimension, but neither my purpose (a light satire on slice-of-life stories) nor my premise (trying to resist change leads only to greater change) demanded an exotic setting.

As a writer with nursery-school drawing skills, I listen first for the character's voice in my mind, delving in and drawing out snippets of speech and personality. Sometimes I'll go so far as to have an in-depth conversation with the burgeoning character. It's a very intuitive, illogical process that might seem a little crazy to an outside observer, but is absolutely crucial for me to hear my characters as they come both plausibly and personably to life. For short stories, I start scripting right away, filling in character details as I write. For longer pieces, however, I often spend days jotting down and revising details of the character's background, emotional make-up and relationships. I call these collections of notes 'character logs' and find them to be invaluable references as I write the script (see page 27 for the script to *Life of Slice*).

Since cartooning is a visual medium, I form a vague physical impression of the character in my mind – not so much the exact likeness, but certainly the signature features, gestures and postures that make the character unique. I will suggest in my script the most essential of my visual impressions, but more often I will let the artist do the heavy lifting of rendering the character into 2D or simulated 3D form. In this case, Patrick Coyle took my few visual cues and turned out some highly expressive character sketches. (In fact, the joy and challenge of this kind of give-and-take collaboration are the main reasons I write comics.)

Another preparative route that is common in animation and long-form comics is for the artist to create a character model sheet. This helps the artist to keep the character drawings consistent in resemblance and proportion as the angles, poses and expressions change. See the example by Jim Zubkavich on this page.

Finally, so as not to underestimate the importance of characters, think for a moment of the cartoons you loved as a child. We may (sadly) forget the name of Charles M Schulz, for instance, or that his half-century-long strip was titled *Peanuts*, but will any of us ever forget Snoopy or Charlie Brown? A cartoonist's greatest legacy is perhaps his or her cast of characters, and digital cartoonists in this new century will be no exception. They will undoubtedly leave us with equally memorable toons.

Below left: **Life of Slice** *characters come to life as initial sketches.*
Below right: *Sketches by Jim Zubkavich for* **The Makeshift Miracle.**

Writing a Storyline

Writing as it pertains to cartooning is a catch-all term that includes dreaming up the ideas, planning out and sketching the sequence of images, and penning the dialogue and narrative captions.

The most common and convenient tool for cartoon writing is the script. Scripts may take any form or format the writer or artist chooses. There are four basic types of script: artist-plotted, sketch, animation and my favourite, full script.

The artist-plotted or 'Marvel-style' script stems from the working methods of Stan Lee and his bullpen of artists from Marvel Comics in the 1960s. Here the artist takes the primary role in storytelling, working from a writer's short plot or one of his or her own, and draws the pages sans text, then gives the finished art to a writer to add dialogue and narrative captions.

The sketch script is exactly what its name implies. The cartoonist writes as she draws, making 'thumbnail' layouts and writing the dialogue and captions in the process of sketching the pictures. Many cartoonists find scripting by sketch to be the quickest and most conducive method for visual storytelling.

The animation script often takes the form of a screenplay and/or storyboard. The format varies from studio to studio. While both animation and comics scripts deal with the movement of the 'camera', the addition of sound, motion and actual time progression makes the animation script move in a way that the comics script only implies.

For my *Life of Slice* comic, I have chosen to use the full-script format. A full script is not unlike a screenplay, though there are some key differences. Rather than breaking a film into scenes, montages, etc., the full script breaks the comic into pages and panels, setting down the dialogue and narration balloon by balloon, caption by caption. The full script has been described as 'a letter from a writer to an artist' and can be friendly or

formal, dashed-off or minutely detailed. If the creative team has other members, then the writer (who may also be the artist) uses the full script to correspond, simultaneously, with the inker, colourist, letterer and editor. In the 'assembly-line' comics industry, where the writer and artist are ordinarily not the same person, full script is the preferred method. In the digital realm, a full script might include screen transitions, scrolling and hyperlink instructions, and sound and animation cues.

There are dozens of great books on storytelling and scriptwriting, among them Will Eisner's *Comics and Sequential Art* and *Graphic Storytelling*, but here are a few tips on writing:

★ Keep it visual.
★ Don't tell in words what you can show in pictures.
★ Space is limited.
★ Don't pack each panel with too many words, or each page (screen) with too many panels.
★ Timing is everything.
★ Guide the reader on a clear path from moment to moment.
★ Use body language.
★ Let your characters speak through physical movement and facial expression as well as through speech.
★ Give it structure.
★ Learn about three-act dramatic structure. Simply put, stories move from the initial setup, through the reinforcement, to the final payoff.

Here is my script for 'Life of Slice'.

···◇ LIFE OF SLICE ◇···

Script by Steven Withrow/Art by Patrick Coyle

PANEL ONE:	NINE-PANEL GRID. BREAK INTO THREE-PANEL PIECES TO FIT THE SCREEN. WE'RE LOOKING IN ON TOM AND NINA, SPENDING A QUIET EVENING IN THE LIVING ROOM OF THEIR CONTEMPORARY LOFT CONVERSION. THEY ARE BOTH IN THEIR EARLY THIRTIES, STYLISH BUT NOT OVERLY SO. TOM IS STANDING, CLEARLY UPSET; NINA IS SITTING CALMLY ON THE SOFA WITH A BOOK. THIS IS A FULL-COLOUR PANEL.
1 TOM:	*Everything's changing.*
2 NINA:	*Changing? How?*
PANEL TWO:	SIMILAR SHOT. SHIFT SUDDENLY TO BLACK-AND-WHITE.
3 TOM:	*It's like my life has lost all colour.*
PANEL THREE:	CLOSE-UP ON TOM. RETURN TO COLOUR. USE PHOTOSHOP TO BLUR HIS IMAGE.
4 TOM:	*I'm nothing but a blur of the man you married, Nina.*
PANEL FOUR:	SAME SHOT. USE SOME WILD FILTER EFFECT TO BLUR TOM'S IMAGE EVEN FURTHER. No dialogue.
PANEL FIVE:	RETURN TO THE SHOT FROM PANEL ONE. TOM AND NINA LOOK NORMAL, BUT THE BACKGROUND HAS CHANGED TO A SCANNED PHOTOGRAPH OF A LUSH TROPICAL LANDSCAPE.
5 TOM:	*Maybe it's not me, you know. Maybe it's the world that's changing.*
PANEL SIX:	CLOSE-UP ON NINA. SHE LOOKS ANNOYED. THE FONTS OF HER WORDS SHIFT FROM NORMAL TO WILD.
6 NINA:	*Goodness gracious, Tom.*
7 NINA:	*Sometimes you make absolutely no sense.*
PANEL SEVEN:	CLOSE-UP ON TOM.
8 TOM:	*Do you want to know a secret?*
PANEL EIGHT:	CLOSE-UP ON NINA. SHE LOOKS INTERESTED.
9 NINA:	*Shoot.*
PANEL NINE:	RETURN TO SHOT FROM PANEL ONE. TOM LOOKS NORMAL, BUT NINA HAS MORPHED INTO A STRANGE PHOTOSHOP CREATION.
10 TOM:	*You're changing, too.*

Sketches

In preparing to draw *Life of Slice*, Patrick Coyle began by reading through my script a few times to get a feeling for the story and to assess its visual challenges. Finding the script to be relatively straightforward, Patrick turned his attention to the characters themselves.

My vision of the characters remaining open, I was pleasantly surprised by the range of personality Patrick was able to give to Tom and Nina in his early sketches. Patrick's line showed a clear, uncluttered style. I got the feeling he knew these two characters as well as I did. I could see our collaboration was already going strong.

To make the strip as believable as possible, Patrick gathered photo references for the characters as well as the background objects (props) that make up the story's setting. He arranged Tom and Nina's living room set, making notes for himself as he drew.

Patrick's next task was to structure the panel layout for the strip from beginning to end. He did a quick layout exercise as a series of small 'thumbnail' sketches, playing with the panel sizes until he found the right arrangement.

Well aware that the artist must direct the reader's eye as it moves across the page or screen, Patrick used guide lines (see the diagonal lines cutting across the panels at right) to help him compose all the visual elements, including the word balloons, on a fluid path from panel to panel. He now had the visual skeleton on which to hang our slice-of-life piece.

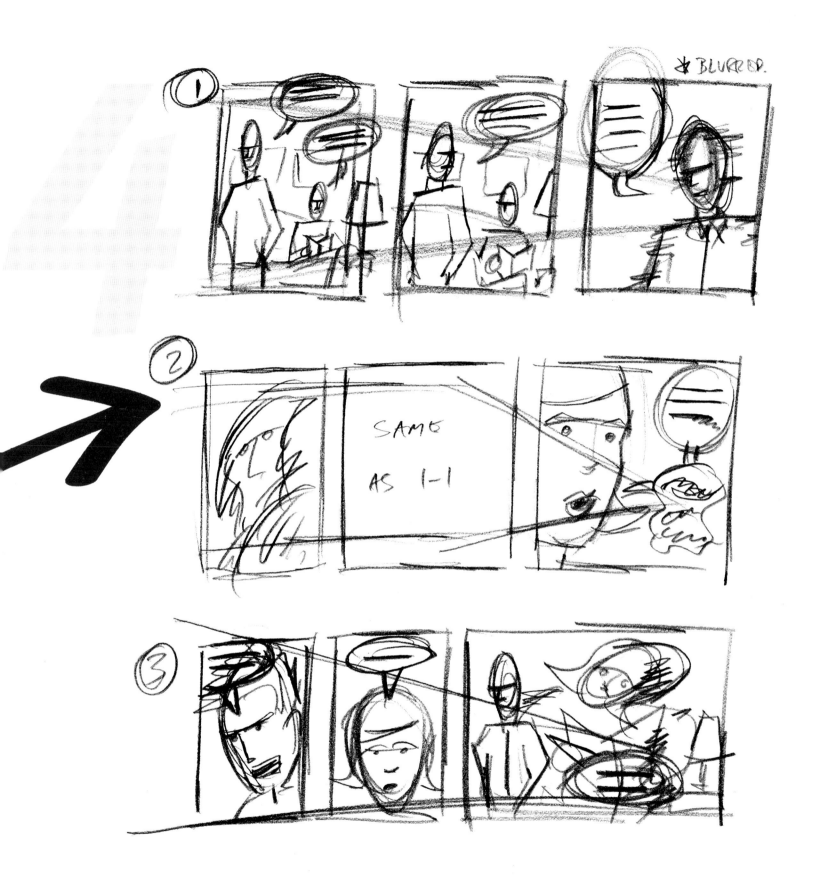

Pencils

While many artists now use digital tools such as drawing tablets and vector-based software to draw their work and never put pencil to paper, Patrick felt more comfortable pencilling and inking *Life of Slice* in the more traditional manner and then scanning the artwork. First, he sketched out the pencils in his sketchbook, leaving them very rough. This is a process that allows him, in his own words, 'to play fast and loose, and to do as many sketches as I want until I like it'.

Next, he traced cleaner, tighter pencils, ready for inking, onto marker paper. In this case, he needed to pencil only three panels, and these could be reused to create the entire nine-panel comic.

This method of 'digital compositing' is now quite common among online and print cartoonists, saving them considerable time and effort without sacrificing the quality of the drawings.

The wonder of digital production!

5a

SAME
BKGD.
AS
'A'

Inks

Patrick opted to ink the comic in two stages, one on paper and the other by computer.

For the paper stage, he used markers to create the outlines and fill in the small areas of black. He marked an 'x' where he needed to fill in the larger areas of black.

To bring his inked pages into the digital realm, Patrick scanned the images at print quality (300 dpi). Using Adobe Photoshop, he increased the contrast so that all the black edges became easy to select and separate from the white background. He then filled in the areas marked with an 'x' to create the final inked version seen at right.

33

Colours, Letters and Effects

In Adobe Photoshop, Patrick placed the inked images into their final positions on the page. He picked a palette of eight colours, which created a tighter, more cohesive look for the comic. Since Photoshop allows multiple layers, he added each colour under the inked layer to create the fully coloured effect.

Using multiple filter effects in Photoshop, Patrick created the special effects in panels three, four and nine. He also dropped in the photograph in panel five.

For the lettering, Patrick exported the colour files as Web-quality images (72 dpi). He then opened them in Adobe Illustrator, which he believes 'creates better lettered images and allows tighter control over them than Photoshop'. He first typed out the line of dialogue, adjusting the text and the line breaks to fit the space available. He then created the word balloon behind it, adding the 'pointer' afterwards. Since the script called for an effect to be added to the type and the word balloons in panel 6, he applied filter effects to that area.

And – voila! – *Life of Slice* was completed. The entire process took Patrick less than three days from the time he received the script.

Editing and Posting

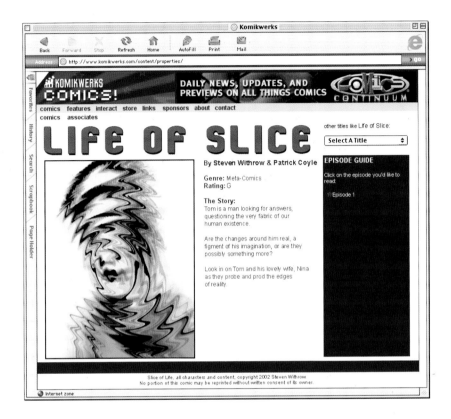

Two often overlooked yet critical steps in the process of creating an online comic are editing and posting.

Editing can take many forms, from gatekeeping and acquisition, through developing a concept and shepherding a project from start to finish, to copy-editing and proofreading. Since *Life of Slice* required little development or organisation, the tasks of copy-editing and proofreading were left to me, the writer. Knowing that unintentional misspellings and grammatical errors can make a well-drawn comic look amateurish, I asked a writer friend to copy-edit my script for me before sending it to Patrick. After the lettered artwork was finished, I proofed the text against my original script, finding no errors or omissions.

The final step, posting, is in some ways the most crucial. If the comic is presented poorly on the screen, then no amount of witty writing or expert artwork will alter the reader's initial perception of the work as a whole and, by extension, the artists who created it.

Being an accomplished Web designer in addition to working as an illustrator, Patrick Coyle had taken the online presentation into account before he put his first pencil line on paper. Breaking the nine-panel strip into blocks of three for ease of viewing on most computer screens, Patrick saved the pages out of Photoshop as 72-dpi JPEG files. He notes that GIF files are good for images that have large, flat areas of colour, but JPEGs are better for detailed images such as those in *Life of Slice*. Patrick designed these eye-catching, easy-to-navigate pages (see opposite) for his site, Komikwerks.com, giving an effective introduction to the comic and suitable space for the comic panels to work their magic.

And there you have it!

behind the scenes with the experts

Technology should never be used just for its own sake when it comes to creating innovative cartoon characters that the audience really cares about. But cartoonists need to understand the unique capabilities that the different technologies offer, in order to get the most out of them.

Characters such as this one have a lifelike feel about them, even if they are obviously fantasy creations in 3D.

Digital technologies have become adept at creating textures and movement with a degree of realism unique to the 3D realm.

Digital cartoonists, I have found, are largely a generous and garrulous lot who view themselves as part of an interconnected global community of artists. A beginning cartoonist can make enormous leaps in his or her development by communicating with fellow artists, collaborating on cartoon projects or simply by sharing art, scripts, links, ideas, techniques and insights by e-mail or on message boards, as well as meeting at conventions and festivals around the world.

This section features interviews and tutorials from accomplished artists who were eager to teach what they have learnt by trial and error. All of the techniques featured here build on basic cartooning, design and computing knowledge. If you are just starting out, you will find dozens of books and online tutorials available on these subjects, all of which can help you develop the fundamental skills. Also, with such a variety of cartoon and comic styles available, there are almost as many methods as there are writers and artists. The ideas featured in this chapter are by no means the only routes to try. What they do offer is a peek behind the curtain at a few common creative processes. They might look mystifying on the surface but, with the right software and a little ingenuity, they are actually quite simple to practise.

On the next few pages you will find useful information on vector-based drawing, creating backgrounds, lettering and colouring in Photoshop, and working with Flash, 3D graphics and animation. If you want to know all the technical detail then you might need to refer to the manual, but every tip and trick shared here came as a result of creative effort and hard-won experience.

Let us join the conversation.

Images on this spread are by Matt Westrup

Toon Typography

Comics and cartoons often combine images and words, and digital tools have begun a worldwide revolution in the arts of lettering and typography. The following is a brief interview with two talented, innovative letterers: Richard Starkings, industry veteran and founder of Comicraft (www.comicraft.com), and Nate Piekos, relative newcomer and founder of Blambot (www.blambot.com).

How would you characterize the letterer's role in comics?

Starkings   Writers are always concerned that the style and placement of the lettering in their books supports the rhythm and pace and tone of their script. I work more closely with writers than artists, although a good letterer must satisfy both creators – nothing spoils a good story more than a badly placed balloon, except perhaps sloppy letterforms. It's the letterer's responsibility to help tell the story and to be as invisible as possible – in much the same way [that] a foley artist, sign painter or sound editor on a movie should be invisible. If you notice sound effects or editing in a movie, most likely it's because they're done badly, and therefore don't feel like a seamless part of the experience. No one can read a comic book as it was intended until it's lettered. The letterer is the first person to read the story as it was intended. He or she has to be conscious of everything the writer wants to say and everything the artist is trying to convey. If the letterforms or balloon shapes and placements don't suit the material, the story could be ruined for everyone.

Piekos   Sometimes I hear people say, 'Well... it's JUST the lettering.' To which I respond, 'Yeah, it's JUST every line of dialogue, every auditory cue, and every written piece of information to develop your plot.' Lettering is pretty important. A good letterer should enhance the design and feel of a book without being so over the top that it stunts the reader's reading process. If we do our job right, you won't even realize we were there! Like a ninja! Font choice and balloon placements do make a huge difference. The fonts should complement and enhance the art. English readers/speakers read left to right, top to bottom. A letterer has to know how the natural flow of the eye will follow through the panels. There's MUCH more graphic design know-how in lettering than anyone thinks. I'd say lettering is about 80% graphic design skill.

Should aspiring digital letterers still bother to learn hand-lettering techniques?

Starkings   I think it's important to understand pen-lettering techniques so that the letterer working on the computer can better appreciate the effects he may be trying to emulate. However, a good graphic designer with a sharp eye probably doesn't need to practise techniques with a pen in order to master them on the computer. The computer is a new tool, and we shouldn't place the restrictions of an old tool on the way lettering and typography might evolve from this moment on.

Piekos   Hand lettering is fading out because of the speed and cost effectiveness of digital lettering, unfortunately. If you're lettering in this day and age, 9 times out of 10, you're doing it on a computer. All the young letterers rave about

the digital lettering companies. But I always say, 'Learn the rules before you try and break them.' Their inspiration should come from the hand letterers. If you don't know who Klein, Workman, Sakai, Rosen or Simek are...don't letter a book until you do. Those guys are the masters.

Which software packages do you recommend for computer lettering?

Starkings   Adobe Illustrator! And our fonts, of course! (http://www.comicbookfonts.com)

Piekos   The industry standard is Adobe Illustrator. I use CorelDraw for very precise perspective work and even for creating my fonts. I build each letter individually in CorelDraw. Once I have an entire set, I move it to Fontographer and adjust the kerning, leading and so on. Then it's a matter of testing, tweaking and saving in the various formats.

Where do you find inspiration for your lettering and designs?

Starkings   We live in a world that is full to the brim with logotypes, letterheads, beautifully designed cigar boxes, orange crates and store signage. Good letterers simply keep their eyes open. Both Marvel and DC created between them a very specific uniform style, which can be traced back to letterers like Gaspar Saladino (now in his 70s and still going strong), Sam and Joe Rosen, Joe Letterese (yes, that's his real name!) and Ben Oda. I've never been happy lettering in one given style, and my personal letterforms, which owe more to Tintin than Superman, were dismissed by my contemporaries as 'too European'. The computer has allowed the limited role of the letterer to grow into the more wide-ranging role of the graphic designer. A handful of pen letterers have responded to the challenge; others have just grumbled noisily and fallen by the wayside.

Piekos   I always try to look outside the comics medium for inspiration. I'm a graphic designer first and foremost, so I'm more interested in design as it relates to the world, not as it relates solely to comics. Americans who are looking to get into any facet of comics tend to be hampered by being influenced only by what is directly around them.

Vector-based drawing

To understand how illustration software works, we must first define the vector. Vector images are made up of scalable, editable objects such as lines, curves and shapes which are defined by mathematical equations. Vectors always render as high-quality images, while the file sizes stay small. You can change the attributes of a vector object freely, using nodes and control points. A key advantage of vectors is that they are resolution independent, meaning you can change the size of the vector image without compromising the quality of the drawing, both on screen and in print. Vector drawings are ideal for cartooning, and the flat 2D appearance has a quality reminiscent of early animation cels.

In a versatile, well-structured progam such as Adobe Illustrator, lines, curves and shapes can be augmented by changes in size, colour and gradient. Scans can be imported as drawing references, and images can be exported to other software programs such as Adobe Photoshop or Macromedia Flash in a variety of file types. Fonts can also be manipulated easily, making Adobe Illustrator useful for comics lettering. Entire cartoons can be created using Adobe Illustrator alone.

POPULAR VECTOR-BASED ILLUSTRATION SOFTWARE

ADOBE ILLUSTRATOR
CORELDRAW
MACROMEDIA FREEHAND
MACROMEDIA FLASH

Left: *Image from demian.5's* When I Am King *showing the range of line weights, gradients and solid colours possible with vector-based drawing software.*

> ❛ *I think there's a lot of potential for these sharp, resolution-independent tools, and I look forward to artists willing to work to their strengths. One artist who seems to be taking advantage of that vector-based clean line is demian.5 from Zurich.* ❜

Scott McCloud (See pages 174 and 175)

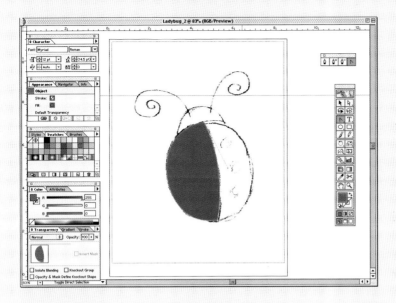

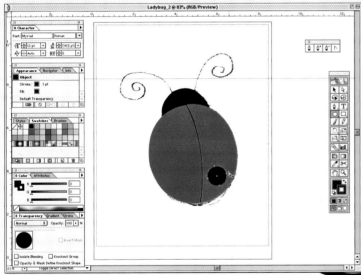

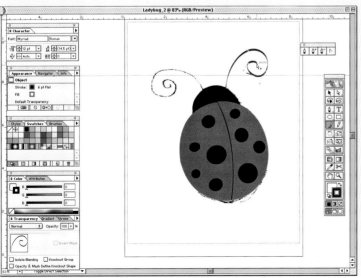

Some Basic Steps for Cartooning in Illustrator (Drawing a Ladybird)

1. Import the scanned image of the ladybird sketch by selecting *File>***Place***.

2. Use the *Pen* tool to create the basic shape of the ladybird's wings.

3. Use the *Convert Anchor* tool to tweak the wing shape to fit the underlying sketch.

4. Select one of the wing shapes and use *Color Palette* to make both *Stroke* and *Fill* red. Repeat for the other wing.

5. Create the head shape using the *Pen* and *Control Anchor* tools and make the *Stroke* and *Fill* black.

6. Use the *Ellipse* tool to create the circles for the dots on the wings. Make *Stroke* and *Fill* black.

7. Copy and paste circles. Use the *Selection* tool to move circles round the wings and to resize the circles.

8. Use the *Paintbrush* tool at the desired width to paint antennae. Make *Stroke* black with no *Fill*.

9. Save file in your desired format.

Pixel-based painting

Paint programs have transformed the art of cartooning throughout the past decade. Pixel-based programs such as Adobe Photoshop, which mimic natural painting tools, are now the primary technology for colouring and visually enhancing comics and animations. In addition, scanned photographs and photorealistic or painterly computer-generated illustrations are now commonplace elements in cartoons, thanks to the photo enhancement and retouching features of paint programs.

Unlike vector-based illustration programs, paint programs are resolution dependent. This is because they use a grid of picture elements or pixels, each with a specific colour value, that combine to create 'bitmap' or 'raster' images. Raster images can give you photo-quality detail, but the image resolution is fixed to the number of pixels present and the image clarity can be lost with any change in size. Also, raster files can be very large, depending on the image size and resolution.

Despite these drawbacks, paint programs can create astonishing visual effects and can manage what would otherwise be tedious and time-consuming manual processes, such as the use of photographic backgrounds, with digital ease and flair. Because these tasks can now be handled more quickly and cleanly by amateurs and experts alike, painting programs can give even a beginner's work a professional polish.

Since the temptation to overdo it is strong with such powerful tools, it takes finesse and restraint, as well as a sense of balance and subtlety, to create truly effective designs. One of the best ways to learn is to study what is being done by others – both in print and online – and then to practise the techniques of layering, colouring, blurring, highlighting and lettering on your own. The *History* palette will be your best friend, as it allows you to undo and redo your trial-and-error paths without wasting materials or time.

POPULAR IMAGE-EDITING SOFTWARE

ADOBE PHOTOSHOP
ADOBE PHOTODELUXE
COREL PHOTO-PAINT
PROCREATE PAINTER
PAINT SHOP PRO

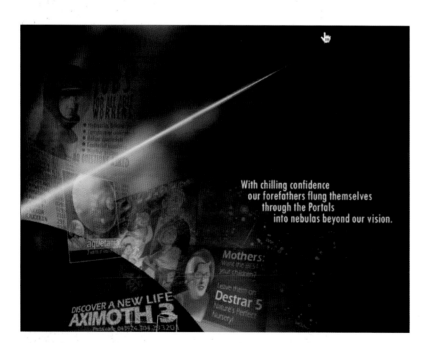

Working with Photoshop has become an essential part of my creative process because it is a forum in which to blend all my wriggling ideas into one cohesive whole. All the sketches and notes and scraps of colours and textures and ideas that have been forming in my mind can be put into Photoshop and can be moved around like a collage, almost always emerging as something more beautiful or startling than what I was expecting. For me, using Photoshop is similar to drawing with a stick dipped in paint, or dripping wax on cloth: although I may end up with something similar to what I was expecting, I will find the process of creation has added elements of surprise and life to the finished piece.

Rigel Stuhmiller
(See pages 142 and 143)

> The act of doing the finished art at this point could be seen as analogous to "pencilling", "inking" and "colouring", but increasingly, the process has become a lot more organic than that. More a background-middleground-foreground approach, and more concerned with continually modifying colour, helping to define planes, and literally "painting with light". Does that make any sense? Basically, the longer I've been doing it, the less like traditional drawing it's become.

Scott McCloud
(See pages 166 and 167)

'My work is unusual in that I draw Argon Zark! entirely on the computer with a Wacom tablet in Painter and Photoshop, rather than scanning drawings done on board and just colouring them on the computer. I also design for the screen rather than the printed page, utilising the RGB colour space, a horizontal format and interactive elements.

'I use a much broader range of image-editing tools and techniques than most comics artists and colour artists (even more than most other digital comics artists). In fact, I indulge in the manipulation of digital images to a greater degree than any other comics artist I'm aware of. (Whether that's good or bad, I don't know.)

'I use the software to help me create fantastic imagery in ways that would be difficult or even impossible in regular drawing. I utilize techniques like the repetition of graphic elements (by copying and compositing); perspective distortion; generated patterns; multi-layered compositing with blending modes like *Darken, Screen* and *Multiply*; transparency masks; colour adjustment layers; texture and pattern generators; manipulated fades and gradients; airbrush painting tools; soft and hard brushes, semi-transparent brushes, brush painting modes, speciality brushes like Painter's *Image Hose*; stroked selections; *Dodge* and *Burn* tools; complex masking; filters that blur, twirl, bend, distort, twist and tile the images; and the interworking of comics drawings with composited 3D renderings and patterns from Bryce. Unlike comics artists creating for print, in which the black plate must be kept separate from the colour plates, I even have the ability to change and manipulate finished "inked" and coloured images.'

Charley Parker
(See pages 118 and 119)

Creating photorealistic backgrounds using Photoshop by Joe Zabel
This portrait of Ray and Finn uses a background and foreground taken from photographs. The original background photograph was taken in daylight. With Photoshop, I did a 'day for night' conversion to it. I coloured over the photo with a grayish-blue tone, using the Paintbucket and Airbrush tools with the Multiply option. The lighted windows were airbrushed opaquely over this. The patches of light on either side of the door were taken from the original daylight photograph, which resided on a layer below the 'night' layer. I simply erased away parts of the 'night' layer to let these patches of light show through.

Ray and Finn were Poser figures positioned in front of this background and lighted to match. The flowers in the foreground were taken from other photographs that had a similar 'day for night' treatment. Each blossom and branch was outlined with the Selection tool, and then the selection was copied and pasted onto a layer above Ray and Finn. As a final touch, part of the flower layer was erased to make it look as if Ray's fingers were curling over the top of the flowers.

Jim Zubkavich on using layers in Photoshop

Seeking an expert opinion on Adobe Photoshop painting techniques, I asked the talented Jim Zubkavich, creator of **The Makeshift Miracle**, *for permission to reprint this helpful tutorial from www.makeshiftmiracle.com.* (See pages 98 and 99)

Learning how to utilize layers in Photoshop can make a huge difference in the quality of your computer-coloured work. Far too many people colour directly on their scanned-in artwork, making revision a huge pain that can be easily avoided. Once you have a good understanding of how layers work, you'll be able to control each aspect of your picture, with much cleaner and stronger results.

1. After scanning in my artwork, I load it up in Photoshop. In this tutorial I'm using Photoshop 6.0, but any version after 4.0 should have similar or identical features to what I'm covering here.

2. If the Layers window isn't already showing, go to Window>**Show Layers** and it will pop up for you. If you hover your mouse over each area, you'll see what each icon does. Actually, you can do that with pretty much any button in Photoshop. Just leave your arrow over the top of something you don't understand, and a little text box will pop up to describe it for you. Easy stuff!

Top: *The initial artwork.*
Left above: *The layers window.* Left below: *Creating a new layer.*
Above: *Painting on layer 1 in normal blending mode.*

3. Currently, our line artwork is called the Background layer. The little padlock icon beside it means that it's locked and is the base layer. The 'Eye' icon means that we're currently viewing that layer. You can view as many layers simultaneously as you want, and by left-clicking on its 'Eye', you can turn on or off the viewing of that layer.

4. When you double-click on the word Background, it'll bring up a separate window called 'New Layer'. Under *Layer Name*, I usually type in Line Art. Naming your layers appropriately helps to keep things organized. Later on, if you've got a dozen or more layers, having clear names helps to keep track of where everything is. From there, click OK, and you'll have changed the locked Background layer to a floating layer called Line Art. Then, click on the *Create New Layer* button, and you should see something like what I've got on the left. You've created a new layer, and now we can add to that layer without wrecking our original artwork. Obviously, the dustbin is for deleting unnecessary layers.

5. If it helps, think of each layer as a pieces of glass laid one on top of another. We can move each layer independently and control the properties of each to create different effects. You can create as many layers as you want and have different elements on each one. You'll notice that the *Blend mode* is set to *Normal* by default. That means that if you highlight Layer 1 and paint on it, it will block out your lines, as seen here.

6. Now, obviously, this is a crappy painting job, but that's not the point. If you click off the 'Eye' icon while Layer 1 is highlighted, you'll see that the original Line Art layer is unharmed. I can paint or erase on this layer (or any other layer) and not harm the others. It's a great way to experiment with different colour combinations or approaches without losing the ability to change it – or discard it by clicking the dustbin icon.

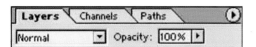

7. It gets better. By clicking on the triangle by the 100%, you can control the transparency of each layer to create ghosting effects. Also, by clicking on the triangle by *Normal*, a list of blend modes comes up. Each has a variety of uses, but I'll just list the ones I most commonly use.

Normal: The default mode. With this, you can paint over the top of mistakes without changing your original work. Use white here and lower that layer's percentage of *Opacity* in order to create glowing, washed-out effects.

Multiply: The mode I use the most. Put your shadows on separate layers with *Multiply*, and they'll blend together with your line art without wrecking the original lines. Most of my shading is done through several layers of the same colour, each put on *Multiply* mode. It gives me total control over how much intensity I need for my shading, in as many stages as I want.

Darken: This mode places your colours only in areas where it is darker than the other layers. It's another way to do shading or to darken areas without needing to be precise while you colour.

Lighten: As with *Darken*, only vice versa. This mode places colours only in areas where it is lighter than the other layers.

8. You can scroll and try all sorts of different modes. If you don't like the effect it creates, scroll to another and try it out. The nice part is that you can always go back and change elements without being afraid of ruining things. Experiment! Try colour combinations and blend modes to your heart's content! That's the great part about Photoshop. Remember to save your work often (with layers intact, Photoshop will save it as a .psd file).

9. Once you're finished and you like what you've got, go to *Layer>**Flatten Image*** and save your work as a .jpg file in order to upload it to the Web. Remember to have your final Web image at 72 dpi (which you can check and alter under *Image>**Image Size***). If you've got Photoshop 6.0, go to *File>**Save For Web*** to make sure your image is a balance of quality and small file size for ideal Web loading.

Whew! That's layers. I hope you found this informative and helpful as you make your own webcomic or do any other colouring in Photoshop. It's a bottomless program with tons of features I'm not even aware of. Never be afraid of simply opening a blank page and experimenting! Most of what I've learned came via online tutorials and my own curiosity.

Now we'll analyse one of my panels and see what layers are used. Okay, here's a panel from *Makeshift Miracle*, page 14. I'll go through each layer, from the bottom through to the top, to explain what it's for.

Sky: *I keep the background (in this case the sky) on a separate Multiply layer from the characters. In some cases, the ground, sky and other background elements are all on different layers. That way, I can colour and change each without interfering with the others.*

Shadows 01, 02, and 03: *My shading is created by putting several layers of flat colour in Multiply mode on top of each other. Even if each layer has the exact same colour, the Multiply mode adds them together and creates stages of shadows in the picture.*

Highlights: *The highlights on the girl's legs are created with this layer on Normal mode. By painting white and carefully erasing the right edge of it, it makes a blended white highlight that is over the top of the Shadows because it's on a higher layer than the Shadow layers. I've also lowered the opacity a bit on this layer so that it isn't as harsh a white tone as the one I started with.*

Line Art: *Notice that the Line Art layer sits in the middle of all the layers. It's on Multiply mode so that the Sky, 3 Shadow and Highlights layers show through. It's placed above those other layers so that I can ensure that the line drawing shows up over the top of all the other colouring. I only place colouring layers above the Line Art layer when I want to wash out the lines with a glowing effect or to correct mistakes.*

Word Balloons 01 and 02: *These are obviously the word balloons. They're in Normal mode so that they sit over the top of the other artwork and colouring. By separating them, I can adjust their placement precisely until I'm pleased with the overall layout.*

Text Layers: *These two layers are the dialogue in the panel. Photoshop 6.0 is great because you can go back and edit text at any point. Often I'll change the wording several times from my original script and see how it looks before finalising it. For dialogue, I use the 12-point DigitalStrip font from Blambot (www.blambot.com) designed by Nate Piekos.*

Borders: *This panel contains the black borders on my panel. I place it at the very top on Normal mode so that it sits over the top of all the other elements.*

Jim Zubkavich on using highlights for depth and drama...

This tutorial expands on what we talked about in the layers tutorial previously, so be sure you understand the basics of using layers and blend modes, as discussed there. Many artists know to add shadows to their work in order to create depth. Shadows help to give a sense of volume and form, and they help to ground a scene. However, few artists pay close attention to the use of light in creating powerful highlights. Through this tutorial, I hope I can alert you to the power of good highlights in creating atmosphere. I've been toying with different colouring techniques on *Makeshift Miracle* as I create my pages each week. I used to start with black-and-white line artwork on a separate layer and add multiple layers of shadows until I'd achieved the effect I wanted. However, I've been getting far more powerful results with an alternate technique.

This sink shot from Makeshift Miracle, *page 22, looks more metallic because of some well-placed highlights. Using the* Polygonal Lasso *tool in Photoshop, I choose shapes that can represent reflected light on the metal. Then, I use a large soft brush and sweep it by the selection area, creating a gradient highlight with a harder reflected edge and a softer spot moving towards the mid tone. So, pick up Photoshop and experiment with highlights. Look at subjects carefully and analyse the light sources and effects all round you.*

Line Art: I start by scanning in my artwork. This panel is from *Makeshift Miracle*, page 27. I also decide what my light source will be. It's important to choose a direction for the light and to think carefully about how that will affect what's round it. Harsh light creates distinct shadows and harsh tone changes; soft light creates more gradients and softer-edged shadows. Do some research. Look to photos, films or other artists and see how they approach light and darkness. Understand how shadows and highlights appear on the subjects you're creating. Reflective metal will have a very different look than a human face or a soft blanket.

Mid-Tone and Shadows: I lay down a mid-tone of whatever colour I choose for this page. The mid-tone becomes a base, literally a midpoint between the shadows and highlights. It keeps me from using too much white in the scene so that I can save it to add drama. The shadows are created by adding layers in *Multiply* mode or by using the *Burn* tool right on the mid-tone layer if I'm in a rush.

Highlights: Here's the punch! I add a new layer on *Normal* mode over the top of the shadow layers but below the line art. Here is where I add white highlights with the brush tool, carefully showing where the harshest light is interacting with the subject. It pulls out much more depth than the typical 'shadows only' picture. It also draws the viewer's eyes towards the rim of light on the character's face. With the highlights on their own layer, I can erase, alter or intensify the highlights without worrying about wrecking the rest of the piece. Looking at stage 2, you can see how much more dramatic the final stage is with the addition of highlights.

...and making word balloons

Many people think of the text and word balloons as the last step in creating their webcomic. It's easy to just want to get the text down and move on to the next panel. But, it's not difficult to create word balloons in Photoshop, and a good set of word balloons can make your stuff look extra spiffy. Photoshop offers you a lot of flexibility to create word balloons and orient them well to present your dialogue. Although I'm using Photoshop 6.0 for this example, 4.0 and 5.0 have nearly everything I'm talking about here and should work just fine. Make sure you plan out your dialogue beforehand. It's really frustrating doing up a nice panel and realising that the words you wanted to put into the panel don't fit. Ideally, all your text should stay the same size, unless characters are yelling or something, so plan ahead and save yourself some problems later on. Type out your dialogue and leave that on a separate layer above the artwork.

Great writing can make a comic incredibly appealing, but only if people can read what you've created. Spend a little time improving your word balloons and it may improve the readability of your comics.

1. Raw Panel: Here's the panel with the art before I add the word balloons. Notice that there's a lot of space for dialogue. I knew that this character would be saying quite a bit, so I planned the space for that. I type out the dialogue and centre it, checking for spelling errors and making sure that it flows well. The nice thing about Photoshop 6.0 is that you can always go back and rework the lettering without having to retype it all.

2. Balloon Build: Using the *Circle Marquee* tool, I create an ellipse that surrounds the dialogue completely. Leave a nice bit of extra space on the sides so that the lettering doesn't jam up against the edges of your balloons. So many amateurs (and some pros) have text jammed up against the sides of the balloon, and it just looks cramped and ugly. Now, with the ellipse selection still there, choose the *Polygonal Lasso* tool. Holding down SHIFT, you'll notice that a tiny + sign appears. That means that we're adding to the selection we've already made with the *Circle* tool. If you click and drag three

times, you can create a triangle-like shape that emerges from the circle and creates the 'tail' for the dialogue balloon. As long as you're holding down SHIFT, you'll have both selected at once. If you're having trouble connecting the end of the polygonal selection to the start to complete it, just double-click and it'll hook up from wherever it is at the start. It may sound complicated here in text, but try it out and it should make more sense. After you've got the selection the way you'd like it, colour it in black with a fill tool or big brush. It will obscure your text once you've covered it, just like in the picture above.

3. Borders & White: Here's the trick for making nice borders on those dialogue balloons. With the area you've just filled in black still selected, go to the menus and click on *Select> Modify> **Contract***. It'll pop up a box asking you how many pixels you wish to contract. I use 2 pixels personally, but you can make it more if you want a thicker outline. The selection will now shrink inwards 2 pixels. Colour in the area that is still selected with white, and you've got your word balloon! Make sure your text is above your Balloon layer and that your artwork is underneath both. Hey presto! You can also use the *Rectangular Marquee* tool the same way to create narration boxes or panels of any shape you want.

4. Finished: I've done a few more selections and created some more balloons for this panel to demonstrate how you can get a bit fancier with it. It can be good to break up a big chunk of dialogue over two balloons like this so that it's easier to read. Look at all sorts of comics to see how they use dialogue balloons to guide the viewer through panels or create interplay in dialogue.

Jim Zubkavich
on digital painting

I've had both good and bad pages in *The Makeshift Miracle* comic, but when stuff comes together well, it's a great feeling. Page 93 was one of those pages. So, I thought I'd do a tutorial outlining how I got to the final image. It was a good learning process for me, and I hope it's helpful to you.

Before you start, make sure that you understand how Layers work in Photoshop. You need to know how layers, layer modes and layer opacity work; otherwise, the techniques below won't help you much.

1. First thing, I did research... I'd never done underwater stuff before, so it was time to learn what it looked like. Whenever I'm not absolutely sure of something, I try to dig up some reference. It's not about copying, but more about understanding what you're trying to represent and seeing trends in it.

Google is great for this. I searched for 'clothed underwater' on Google's Web and image search and gathered about 30 pictures showing how clothes look underwater, as well as giving me ideas on bubble patterns.

2. From there, I drew the line art, trying to incorporate what I had seen, but not copying. I figured that the back leg and arm would be blurred out or obscured with bubbles, so there would be no point in painstakingly drawing it if it would just get wiped out.

3. Because I do the pages in monochromatic tones (one-colour), I tend to do them as greyscale images and add a layer with a *Color* blend mode to 'dye' everything beneath. That allows me to change the overall colour without messing with each layer.

My original line art scanned in.

A dark grey layer on Multiply used for a base tone.

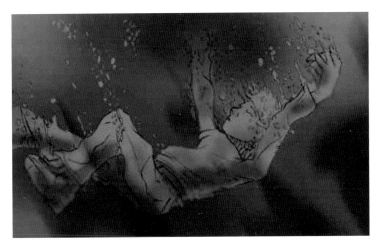

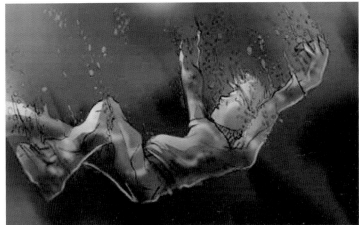

4. I dropped in a mid-tone of medium to dark grey on *Multiply*, giving me a solid base from which to build shadows down and highlights up. I almost always use a mid-tone, but in this case it was especially dark because I knew that the final image would be a dark underwater scene.

5. I added shadows with layers on *Multiply*, trying to keep in mind where my light source was and what effect I wanted. I also added in the blue *Color* layer, so I could see what it would look like finished, even though I was still working in greys underneath.

6. The water effects are done with areas highlighted with the *Polygonal Lasso* coloured dark, and then they're *Gaussian* or *Motion* blurred. Then, I lowered the *Layer Opacity* of the layers

Above left: Various layers on Multiply *for shadows.*
Above right: Various layers on Normal *for highlights.*

Bubble and blurred streak layers added in. Finished!

to make them more transparent. It's easier to paint darker and lower the *Opacity*, I find, than to paint them as mid-tones and possibly wish they were darker later.

7. The most important step for high-contrast lighting like this is the highlights. The shadow layers are done with *Multiply*, but the highlights are various Layers done on *Normal* mode, sitting on top of the shadow layers. I picked out areas with the *Polygonal Lasso* and swept my brush over them to create *Gradients*, rather than using the clunky *Gradient Fill* tool.

Once again, layer *Opacity* is your friend here… I painted heavy white and used *Opacity* to tone it down to the level I wanted. That way, I could always up the intensity of it without repainting areas. The more layers you can handle, the more control of individual areas you can get. These highlights are spread out over six layers.

8. Now for the crazy part, the bubbles. I made five layers of various circular blobs, motion-blurred streaks and speckled bubble trails, all on *Normal* mode, sitting over the top of the other highlights. Some of the layers are above the *Line Art* layer so that they overlap it (check the bubbles from his mouth).

It wasn't exactly this simple a progression. I went back to add more *Shadow* layers several times and went back and forth quite a bit to get the right effect. Still, these 'steps' should be helpful for a start.

Flash animation

'With the new tools, animation could almost be filtered down to its true essence: the display of movement. The only "illusion" now is the separation of the viewer from the world of the screen (we're not creating truly three-dimensional kinetic mechanisms). The wonderful thing about Japanese anime that translates so well online is its simplicity of movement. Rather than creating and transitioning through many single frames, the illustrator creates a single frame that displays the character's movement and emotion. The background colours are blurred and shifted to create the illusion of motion as the character "slides" through a frame. That's why an anime-inspired style seemed such a natural choice for Flash animation and for Broken Saints itself.'

Brooke Burgess (See pages 112 and 113)

'Digital animations are currently a more successful use of the Web than online comics. Flash has made it easy for experimentation with styles of animation. Animators with no formal training have been extremely creative with the tools at hand and have made some beautiful pieces. Flash animations have begun to emulate film and TV (although they are restricted by bandwidth requirements and constrained to a more limited palette). But the Web's main strength, and what can set it apart from all other current media forms, is its power of real-time interactivity. Tapping into this power is what will evolve webcomics and animations from emulations of current media.'

Rigel Stuhmiller

Imagine if the entire multifaceted process of frame-by-frame animation could be compressed into a single, simple-to-use digital application. This is exactly what Macromedia Flash offers the animation storyteller. With Flash, you find a world of timelines, keyframes, tweens, onion skins, layers, mattes, fade-ins, composites, colours and sounds.

Today, many cartoonists are discovering the great flexibility of Flash for character and scene animation. Results vary, but a determined animator can now produce movie-quality results at home without a huge budget or large production team.

Flash is a fairly complex tool, and there are many great books that discuss all the ins and outs of using it, including *Flash Character Animation Applied Studio Techniques* by Lee Purcell (Sams Publishing, 2002). I'll give only a few expert perspectives on Flash, along with a brief overview of the creation of *Broken Saints* (see facing page), one of the mostly highly acclaimed Flash movies worldwide.

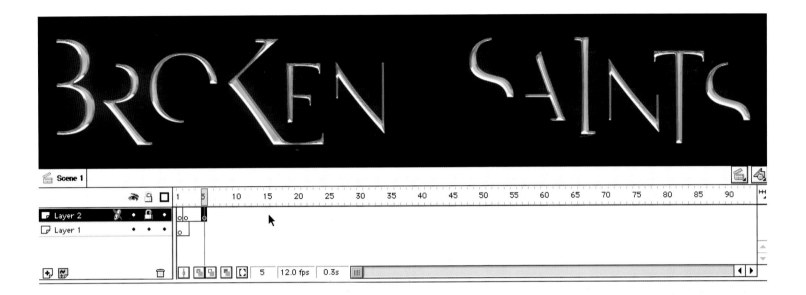

Creating Broken Saints — by Brooke Burgess

1. A shotlist (between 100 and 150 shots) is created as an outline for a chapter.

2. Rough storyboards for the shots and transitions are created on paper, with technical and time limitations debated, art styles proposed and cuts/additions taking place.

3. 'Pencils' of the characters are created using a Wacom tablet and Painter.

4. All subsequent additions will be created on other 'layers' within software to allow for versatility in post-production.

5. After checking the basic composition of the pencils, the characters are 'inked' and cleaned up on the computer.

6. Flat paints are then added, followed by basic shading and highlights.

7. After looking at the paintings in progress, the backgrounds are created in Painter and Illustrator.

8. Photoshop 7 is used to adjust lighting, highlights, shading and tone of the characters and backgrounds.

9. Character and backgrounds are fused in the Flash authoring tool.

10. Effects tests are performed to gauge any frame-rate difficulties during animations or transitions. Any opportunity to use lower-resolution artwork to save overall file size is considered here.

11. A general timeline (i.e., first edit in Flash) is created for the chapter with a first pass on shot placement, 'camera' movements, effects and transitions.

12. Specific dialogue/text is written for all scenes and positioned/timed in the chapter.

13. Music loops and effects are created/edited in SoundForge and then compressed for Flash.

14. Multiple performance tests of the final cut on slower machines are performed to gauge timing and intensity. Scenes that cause 'bogging' (major frame-rate drops) are re-worked and tested.

15. The finished chapter is released to a hungry fanbase!!!

3D graphics and animation

'The CG animation I've done has been 3D. I pose the character out in keyframes, similar to how I work traditionally, and I manipulate the computer to tween the poses the way I intend the character to move. The keys aren't drawn; they are virtual 3D. I've seen 2D drawings that computers have tweened and haven't liked the results. The computer can't see the implied dimension of the drawing, so it just inbetweens lines, not forms – like a really bad human assistant animator.'

Chris Bailey
(See pages 110 and 111)

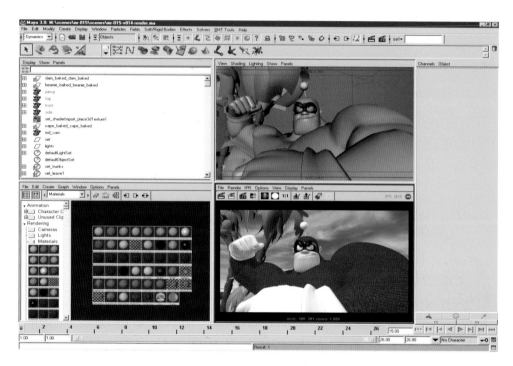

From storyboarding and directing to modelling and rigging, 3D computer graphics (CG) animation skills are some of the most difficult to master, and competition for work in the animation, movie, commercial production and videogame industries can be fierce. Still, thousands of young hopefuls enter the field each year, while others are content to show their independent short films at animation festivals.

Bill Fleming, a pioneer of 3D photorealism and author of several books on 3D animation, gives this advice: 'Don't get frustrated. At first, things will be terribly daunting, but in time it will become second nature. Far too many people jump into this industry hoping to master 3D overnight, but it takes time, years in fact. The technology is also rapidly evolving, so you must stay on top of new developments constantly. This isn't an easy business, but it can be highly rewarding.'

POPULAR 3D SOFTWARE

MAYA
3D STUDIO MAX
LIGHTWAVE
ANIMATION:MASTER
BRYCE

'The problem with technology is it can greatly simplify some tasks while greatly complicating others. For example, the advent of bones for posing characters was great, except for the fact the bones created countless deformation problems, like weight maps that assign specific points to a bone, but then that technology was crude at first. Now, of course, it has evolved to become a solid tool, though it is still not a complete solution, so now we use Expressions to apply morphs to joints to combat deformation problems that even weight maps didn't solve. Well, Expressions are more like scripting/programming, so now there is another skill to master. As you can see, a solution creates another problem, which is solved by a solution that spawns yet another problem. In 2D, the animator simply draws the body perfectly and doesn't have to worry about technology getting in the way or falling short. Being a digital animator means also being a technical engineer and in many cases a programmer. It can be very daunting.'

Bill Fleming

Gil Agudín on 3D design

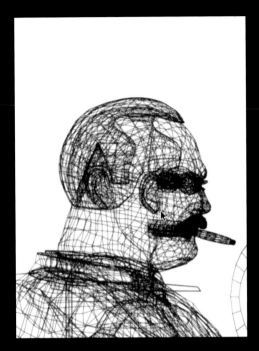

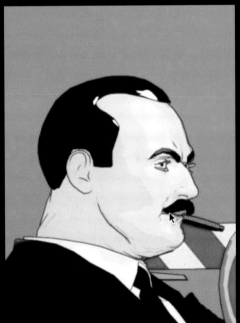

'I'm fascinated by non-photorealistic rendering, in particular all those techniques that can render 3D scenes in styles that make them look hand drawn (toon shading or toon rendering). For me, computer graphics are not an end but a means – a tool that you use as you use your pencil or your brush.

'Why is almost everyone trying to make images that look just like the real world? There was a time when painting also tried to be just like reality to the most minute detail (academic style). The academic works were so perfect and so cold at the same time. But with the arrival of photography, painting was freed and new ways of expression appeared (Impressionism, Cubism, Surrealism). Then all the Monets, Van Goghs, Picassos and Dalis erupted.

'I wonder what is going to happen the day that computer art abandons photorealism.'

1. Tools:
3D Studio Max
Character Studio
CartoonReyes

I start with a 3D model. I set characters, lights, and camera.

2. I assign textures and materials from CartoonReyes. I use this render as a reference for the final hand drawing.

3. I generate a second render. This time with no contour lines. I'll use it as my colour plate.

4. At last, I merge the hand drawing with the colour plate. The result is another frame from my comic book, The Underdog.

Mike Brown on creating walk cycles

' The technique that follows was inspired by techniques from the book The Animator's Survival Kit *by Richard Williams. If you find this tutorial useful, I highly recommend you pick up a copy. We're going to use a pose-to-pose method to animate today's walk. At 24 frames per second, a walk will usually range anywhere from 8 frames per stride for a brisk pace to 16 frames for a leisurely stroll. To be clear, I'm going to animate at 24 frames per second and make each stride 12 frames (march time). '*

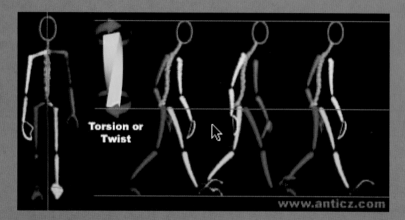

1. Let's begin by animating a walk with the contact poses. This is basically mid-stride where the heel strikes the ground. Contrary to what you might think, this is the part of a walk that has the least amount of weight. It's the pose directly after this, or the down pose, that sells the weight. But we'll get to that later. For now, let's concentrate on this pose. Go ahead and pose every part of your character on frame 1. Make sure the forward leg striking the ground is straight (knee is not bent); otherwise, your character may look as if he's carrying a load in the back of his trousers. Also, make sure you add a little vertical torsion in the hips and shoulders (i.e., twist the torso slightly). Now advance the time 12 frames (frame 13) and do the the next heel strike pose. Remember to key everything on your character. The final heel strike pose will happen 12 frames later on frame 25.

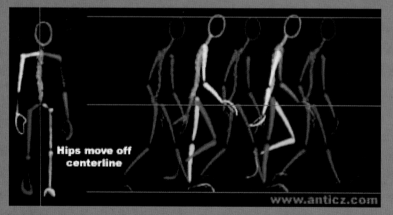

2. Now that we have the contact poses set, let's start breaking it down by adding the passing poses. Go to frame 7 and pose every part of your character in a passing pose. Make sure to keep the shoulders and hips in opposition to each other and drop the shoulder and hips laterally (i.e., curve the torso slightly).

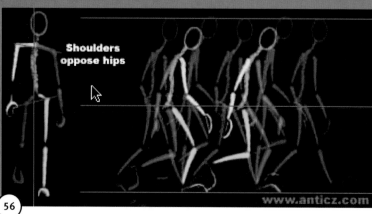

3. Now our walk is starting to take shape. Once you get this far, the rest is a breeze. As long as the contact and passing poses work, you can do just about anything you want with these breakdown poses and it will work. For now, we're just going to animate a generic walk. Let's break it down further by adding the actual weight-bearing pose (down pose) between the contact and passing poses (frame 4). The forward knee drops and bends, the head shifts forwards, and the hips and shoulders tilt. (Don't forget to key everything on your character, or one pose might wind up affecting a pose you've already worked out.)

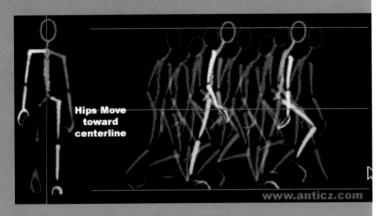

Hips Move toward centreline

www.anticz.com

4. Now we'll add the striding or up pose between the passing and contact poses (frame 10). This is where your character bounds upwards and begins to fall forwards. The hips begin moving back towards the centreline so that the body is ready to catch itself with the opposing foot.

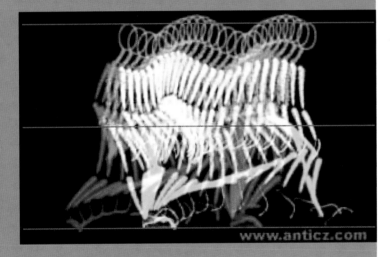

www.anticz.com

5. We're almost finished. Now it's time to go back and inbetween everything. In your curve editor, you'll want to smooth out any nasty bumps or ledges in your curves. You'll also want to make sure you've got a nice steep hard-edged curve for the heel striking the ground. At this point, the walk is pretty much finished. I like to go through and offset keys on overlapping joints to loosen up everything and give it a more natural feel. Also, make sure frame 1 and frame 25 match up perfectly. When you're all done, you should wind up with a nice looping walk cycle between frames 1 and 24 (frame 25 is a repeat).

Using this technique, anyone can achieve convincing walk cycles of all types. Now that you've completed a faily generic walk, you might try animating the following types of walks: a sneaky walk, a feminine walk, a strut, a sad walk, a drunk walk, a goofy walk, etc. Good luck, and happy animating!

Good-old 2D or 3D CG?

Raf Anzovin Look at the animation of Stitch in Disney's *Lilo and Stitch* (2002). Most of the movements he makes wouldn't really work if you tried to duplicate them in CG. It has too much 'weight' to it, too much expectation of reality to do something so completely outlandish. I think traditional animated features are going to get more stylized, more zany and rely more on the sly warping and breaking of reality that's possible with the traditional approach.

On the other hand, if you want to see where CG animation is going, look at the animated characters in Lucasfilm's *Star Wars: Attack of the Clones* (2002). These creatures look very 'real'. In fact, Lucasfilm clearly wanted to make sure that the audience could see not just their gross body motion but also their muscles sliding and rippling under the skin, and the jiggle of fat round their bones. This is just the latest example of an obvious trend – animators want their digital characters to look real. Sometimes this can get in the way. We've all seen examples of very well-modelled, realistically textured characters who wear their realism like a dead weight. The animators got so bogged down in the minutiae of movement that they missed the important part – the sense of awareness and character, the 'illusion of life'. But in *Attack of the Clones*, instead of allowing the realism of the characters to bog them down, the animators used it as a way to make the characters seem even more alive.

Someone once asked me what the point was to animating characters in a fight sequence or a complex dance by hand, when you could just as easily motion capture or rotoscope real martial artists or dancers and save yourself the trouble. The answer is that a digital animator who has gone beyond the basic skill level of moving the character around in a believable way, and who understands how to imbue movement with a sense of character and thought, can make the character seem alive and full of energy in a way that no human being really is. It's like comparing a Rembrandt painting to a photograph of that same painting. The photograph shows 'reality', but the Rembrandt original leaps off the canvas at you in a way the photograph can't. Digital animation hasn't reached anywhere near this potential yet. In fact, I don't think the best digital animators have yet caught up to the master animators like Bill Tytla, Milt Kahl or Glen Keane. But I think that's where digital animation is going.

Locks on the digital door

This book deals mainly with the positive aspects and 'open doors' of digital cartooning. But there are still many barriers in the digital cartoonist's way. Although there are numerous fixes being proposed and tested each day by creators, designers, programmers and marketers, there is no skeleton key to open every locked door. Of course, trying to define and suggest solutions for even the most common challenges and issues is beyond the scope of this book, so I have opted to list some of the primary concerns that digital cartoonists have voiced to me in my research. Fortunately, a new generation of artists has accepted the creative challenge and may end up changing far more than simply the surface 'look and feel' of cartoons. They might just alter the course of visual art for ever.

Technical Difficulties

'How do we keep pace with – and afford – the initial investment in, and constant upgrades to, computer hardware and software?'

'How do we train ourselves in the creative use of new hardware and software?'

'Will we ever have a monitor or other viewing device that is as readable, durable and portable as a book?'

'When will high-speed broadband connections become the norm for Internet users?'

'How do we create cartoons that are not tied to a specific browser, plug-in or modem speed?'

'How do we keep file sizes small enough for fast downloads without sacrificing image quality?'

'How do we store our files so that we can keep permanent archives of our work?'

Creative Difficulties

'How do we expand the form and create digital cartoons that do not replicate what already works in print and movies?'

'How do we attract new readers to our work from a content standpoint?'

'Does the digital cartoonist still need to learn and practise traditional drawing skills in addition to digital skills?'

'How do we design websites and cartoons that take advantage of the interactive capability of the Internet?'

'Does adding limited animation and sound turn your comic into a cheap imitation of animated movies?'

'How do we protect our copyrights when we post our work online?'

Economic Difficulties

'How do we make a living – or even recoup our investment – from Web comics and animation?'

'How do we attract new readers to our work from a marketing and sales standpoint?'

'Will there ever be a viable economic model for online cartoons?'

'Should we go it alone or join a studio, corporation or anthology site?'

'What marketing and payment methods should we choose to drive traffic to our sites? Banner ads? Subscriptions? Micropayments?'

'How do we avoid "the success tax" if our site traffic suddenly spikes?'

'Are online cartoons just a feeder market for more "legitimate" industries such as print comics and Hollywood movies?'

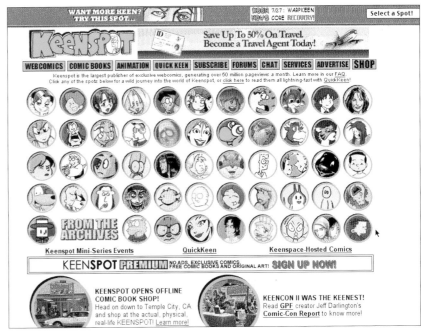

Above: *Joey Manley's Modern Tales* (www.moderntales. com) is home to some of the world's most innovative digital cartoonists, and the site is one of a handful that are succesfully pioneering the subscription payment model. As of September 2002, Modern Tales has also branched out into two sister sites, www.adventurestrips.com and www.serializer.net.

Above right: *Keenspot* (www. keenspot.com), founded in 2000 by Chris Crosby and Darren Bleuel, is a premium service that presents many of today's most popular online comic strips.

In the late 1990s, Steve Conley created and promoted a method he called 'tooncasting' to market and distribute the online version of his comic *Astounding Space Thrills* (see pages 116 and 117). The tooncasting model has since been adopted by several other influential digital cartoonists, including Indigo Kelleigh, Greg Hyland and Marty Baumann. Conley told *The Comics Journal,* 'Astounding Space Thrills is distributed via "tooncasting", which means it uses the Web as a broadcast medium for comics. It markets itself. The idea of tooncasting is a reversal of the common Web methodology. Most websites are based on the notion of having the user visit every day. The reader has to come to you.

I make it so readers don't have to come to me. They have to come to me to read the previous episodes, but to see what happened today, they can visit any one of 3000 webpages.'

61

CHAPTER ONE

A SHOWCASE OF THE BEST FUNNIES IN THE BUSINESS

toon hilarities

Where would cartoons be without humour? When laughter is the object of art, the cartoonist draws on a keen sense of timing, a knack for exaggeration and a delightfully delicate rendering of character.

Whether satirical, nonsensical or downright bizarre, cartoon humour is as much a part of modern culture as the telephone or the morning newspaper. Who hasn't broken into hysterics while following Snoopy's Red Baron behind enemy lines, or chuckled uncontrollably at the animal antics of Bugs Bunny and Daffy Duck? There's no doubt that humour is one genre – or is it a mood that runs through many genres? – that will never go out of style.

Master comedians such as Buster Keaton and Charlie Chaplin have taught us that the foremost element of all humour is an impeccable sense of timing. So it should come as no surprise that cartoons, a medium rooted in the most minute particulars of pace and rhythm, are natural vehicles for guffaw-inducing gags and whimsical witticisms. Now the big question for digital creators is: Can your computer make you funny? That's about as likely as waiting for your car to drive you to work, so something else is needed.

No one is quite certain whether having a sense of humour is a learnt skill or an innate talent. Comedic tastes are as difficult to decipher as tastes in music or food. However, it is interesting that we rarely laugh unless someone has done or said something funny or something funny has been done to some person. So, we laugh at each other, at ourselves and, for some reason, we are also fond of laughing at animals. The more like humans they are, the more laughable they seem to us. We hardly ever laugh at rocks or rainclouds or trees.

So what does this mean for novice cartoonists? Simply put, comedy is a function of character, and humour has no force if it is not somehow personified – made human, in other words.

For a front-row seat at humorous cartooning at its digital best, take a look at the various approaches the cartoonists in this section have taken to make us laugh.

Left & far left: *Pages from Dorothy Gambrell's* Cat and Girl *and* The New Adventures of Death.

roberto corona

' *I'm not a pioneer in terms of technology: I keep it as simple as possible. I don't want someone not to be able to read my stuff because they have the wrong browser or Flash plug-in.* '

'I use the computer to composite pencils from multiple images and do extensive touch-up and revisions on screen. I'll copy and paste whole characters rather than draw them twice. I print faint blue-line copies to ink. All colour and text are digital. Prior to using the computer, I had no means of colouring, as I can't paint or use marker pens with any kind of skill.

'The Web has been critical in giving me a means to self-publish for zero cash investment. I had often thought of printing my own books, but the costs were always too intimidating (as was the prospect of hawking the stuff myself).

'Web publishing also affords an editorial position that I find very liberating (i.e., there isn't one!). Although I always enjoyed working with hands-on, over-the-shoulder type editors in print, my current work is too personal for that kind of third-party workover.'

COUNTRY:
NEW ZEALAND

SITE ADDRESSES:
WWW.KOMIKWERKS.COM
HTTP://GLOBALBOB.CJB.NET

HARDWARE:
IMAC, FLATBED SCANNER, EPSON STYLUS C40 PRINTER

SOFTWARE:
ADOBE PHOTODELUXE, ADOBE ILLUSTRATOR

'I like to think of Welcome to Heck *as "victimless humour".'*

The satirical Too Much Coffee Man *has a large fanbase, both in its print and online forms.*

'I'm sloppier now. I know I can fix it later on the computer. If I'm running late, I'll letter on the computer, too.'

COUNTRY:
US

SITE ADDRESSES:
WWW.TMCM.COM
WWW.LIVEJOURNAL.COM

HARDWARE:
'I PENCIL, INK AND LETTER THE
TRADITIONAL WAY (BY HAND). I USE
THE COMPUTER TO COLOUR AND TO
FIX MULTIPLE MISTAKES.'

SOFTWARE:
ADOBE PHOTOSHOP, ADOBE
ILLUSTRATOR, QUARK XPRESS,
MACROMEDIA FLASH

shannon wheeler

' *Digital comics is just another medium that I use and enjoy.*

It's the message that's ultimately important. My message is "don't worry, be

happy". Wait, sorry, that's just a song that's playing on the radio. '

jonathan rosenberg

' The Web allows me to circumvent traditional publishers and bring my work directly to the public. I can find a niche audience and fill a void that wouldn't have been catered to previously. It allows me to keep my publication costs low, as I don't have to deal with printing. I also don't have to deal with editors diluting and compromising my work. '

COUNTRY:
US

SITE ADDRESSES:
WWW.GOATS.COM
WWW.MODERNTALES.COM

HARDWARE:
DELL WIN2K PC, CANOSCAN N656U,
WACOM TABLET, PALM V

SOFTWARE:
ADOBE PHOTOSHOP, MACROMEDIA
FIREWORKS, ADOBE ILLUSTRATOR

'I've always worked on computers, so I've always considered them to be an essential part of what I do. I've made better use of them over time, however. I now use a font to letter *Goats* directly in Photoshop, which means I save time and it looks cleaner and more consistent than it used to. I also enjoy how Photoshop allows me to clean up my lines after I've scanned in the artwork, and I wouldn't be able to do the colouring for *Patent Pending* without it.'

Pages from the wildly irreverent comic strip Goats, *one of the longest running and most popular online strips.*

roger langridge

'*The computer has allowed me to use colour liberally without worrying how I'll be able to afford to print it; it's encouraged me to be productive (a weekly strip and all that); it's enabled me to sharpen certain satirical effects by putting typefaces and professional layout tools at my disposal. On the downside, it's given me a reason to be lazy about the crosshatching and hand-lettered calligraphy which used to be my trademark.*'

COUNTRY:

UNITED KINGDOM

SITE ADDRESSES:

WWW.MODERNTALES.COM
WWW.HOTELFRED.COM

HARDWARE:

MACINTOSH IBOOK

SOFTWARE:

ADOBE PHOTOSHOP, ADOBE ILLUSTRATOR

'The current state of the Web might best be described as "chaotic" – but that's partly what's so good about it; anybody can do whatever they want. Unfortunately, that's also what's wrong with it. I hope the "shake-down" period takes as long as possible, though; in a world where our entertainment is largely spoon-fed to us by multinational corporations, anything that allows different voices to be heard is a good thing, even if 99% of those voices are squawking gibberish. The remaining one percent make it worthwhile.'

COUNTRY:
US

SITE ADDRESS:
WWW.BOXJAMSDOODLE.COM

HARDWARE:
PC, SCANNER

SOFTWARE:
ADOBE PHOTOSHOP DELUXE

boxjam

❛ *As print newspapers take their eventual place beside papyrus scrolls, digital comics will be the only comics show in town. At that point, some webtoons will become full-time jobs for creators, as Internet publications are willing to pay them for exclusive rights, but there will still be a flood of available "amateur" toons for any taste.* ❜

'I see myself, in immodest moments, as sort of "The Ramones" of webcomics. Several cartoonists have told me their decision to do a webtoon was due to seeing my comic. I think that's because my work reminds people there's nothing to be intimidated by here – it's just goofy drawings and funny writing. If BoxJam can do this, why can't anybody? I don't mean that in a self-deprecating way, but I remind people that simple is not bad, and that if you want to do this, there's nothing stopping you.'

'I have always approached *BoxJam's Doodle* as a Web being. Some early decisions were based on that, including that I change its size every day, have a very loose structure that allows for whatever visual composition I want, and never stop to consider how this could be printed during the creation process.

'I don't worry about fitting drawings into a certain box; I make drawings whatever size I want, sans borders, and work out the composition digitally.'

Above and left: *BoxJam's minimalist style and do-it-yourself sensibility have enticed many newcomers to join the webcomics scene.*

andrew willmore

' *The Web is an excellent way to get your name and your work out there at little or no cost. With luck, you could build a following and test reaction to your material before investing insane amounts of money in a self-publishing venture or something of that nature.* '

'Although I'm sure digital media will continue to play a larger and larger role both in our daily lives and our chosen forms of entertainment, the print media, television and other popular standbys aren't going anywhere anytime soon. I believe digital comics and cartoons will gain in popularity, but digital comics will never replace tangible, print comics you can keep in a collection. Each medium has its own place; neither should overtake the other.'

COUNTRY:
US

SITE ADDRESSES:
WWW.STUDIOBUENO.COM
WWW.KOMIKWERKS.COM

HARDWARE:
DELL DIMENSION

SOFTWARE:
ULEAD PHOTOIMPACT

STUDIO BUENO

'Doubtless the creators of online comics will be the superstar celebrities of tomorrow, living exuberant lives marked by money and power. Or if that's asking too much, perhaps we can at least look for the medium to continue to expand with a growth in the variety and quality of online comics.'

Angel Applebee, Bueno, Fatback & Skinny McLean (c) 2002 Andrew Willmore

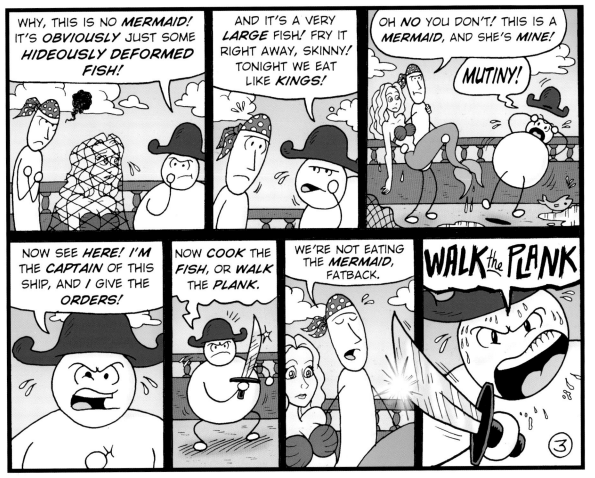

Left: *Willmore on his* Fatback and Skinny McLean: *'I'm just putting out my own warped brand of cartoons that will hopefully bring a smile and a bit of entertainment to someone's day.'*

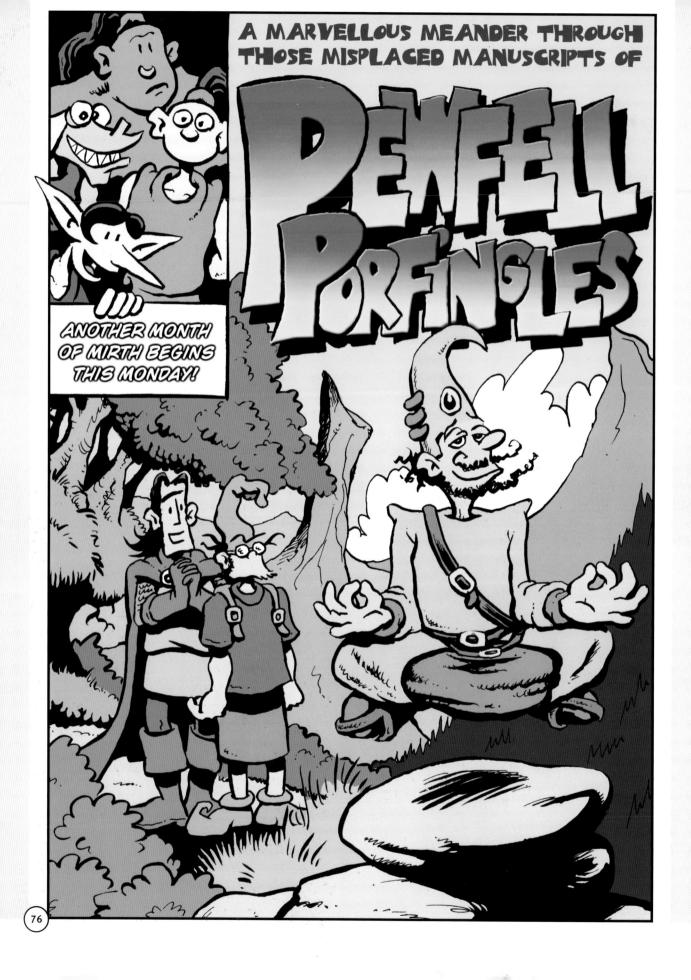

chuck whelon

'*The Weird Worlds of Pewfell Porfingles* is a long-form adventure serial that also works as a gag-a-day strip. It is drawn as a full page of up to six panels, currently updates with a new page every weekday and is in colour. The strip chronicles the adventures of Pewfell, the world's worst wizard. It is set in a fantasy world, using common role-playing game themes and characters, but it has a definite domestic twist. Characters are based mainly on people I know, and, believe it or not, situations are often derived from my own everyday experiences.'

'Comics, like most other things on the Web, are still in a highly developmental state. For the most part, they are produced in much the same way as in the past, and I suspect most webcomic artists still ultimately aspire to see their work in print. However, artists are actively exploring the new tools they have, such as digital production techniques, 3D rendering and the infinite canvas. So in much the same way as the first arthropods must have emerged from the sea to colonize the land, the world of comics is being revolutionized!

'One area I would personally like to explore more with *Pewfell* is the interactive nature of the strip, and I'm hoping to work with some readers who are also game fans to develop some role-playing features for the strip.'

COUNTRY:

US (BORN AND RAISED IN UK)

SITE ADDRESSES:

WWW.PEWFELL.COM

WWW.MODERNTALES.COM

WWW.WHELON.COM

HARDWARE:

MAC, SCANNER, DRAWING TABLET

SOFTWARE:

IMAGE EDITOR/TYPESETTER

Left: *A still from one of Loeck's lively animated musical pieces featuring Raymond the Mouse and his beloved cheese.*

Right: *Just a small selection of characters created by Loeck and Taylor. 'My animation,' Taylor says, 'makes kids laugh, sing or dance. Basically my work makes people smile!'*

michael loeck & jason taylor

'The computer has improved my workflow and has made it easier to put my ideas on the screen rather than redrawing the same scene twice. The Web has definitely made it easier to find creative inspiration without running to the library on a daily basis. It helps with problem solving to know there is this mass of people that run into the same problems along the way. Questions can be answered a lot more quickly.'

Michael Loeck

'The computer is essential for my form of animation. It allows me to create my animation in a flexible and affordable way. The Web has played an enormous role in getting my work seen by people around the world. It has made distribution easy. The Web allows me to create a viewing environment for my work. My webpage sets the mood for the animation and allows the viewer to immerse him- or herself in my world. Without the Web, a great deal of today's popular cartoonists and animators would still be unknown to the general public.'

Jason Taylor

COUNTRY:
US

SITE ADDRESSES:
WWW.IMMORTAL3D.COM
WWW.BOUNCYTALES.COM
WWW.HI-FI-LO-FI.COM/TAYLOR

HARDWARE:
DUAL PROC PENTIUM III ZEON 55 PC, ATHLON 900

SOFTWARE:
3D STUDIO MAX, ADOBE PHOTOSHOP, ADOBE PREMIER

RAYMOND

SHOOMAX

CLYDE

> *All my work is produced at least partially using my computer as a tool, and eventually, when the technology is good enough, I will probably dispense with paper and pens. Remember that the computer is just a tool. Digital comics are not "made by computers"; they are still produced by people.*

craig conlan's
hairy mary

short stories from the world of hairy mary

short cuts

COUNTRY:
UK

SITE ADDRESSES:
WWW.CRAIGCONLAN.COM

HARDWARE:
IMAC, WACOM TABLET, UMAX SCANNER

SOFTWARE:
ADOBE ILLUSTRATOR, ADOBE PHOTOSHOP, ADOBE STREAMLINE, MACROMEDIA FLASH

Above : *Images from Conlan's versatile and vivid cartoons. He notes a range of influences, including British humour and Japanese culture.*

'I prefer comic-strip stories to be in some way finite. A story has a beginning, middle and an end, right? I mean, Superman comics will still be around after I'm dead, and ongoing series have their place, but they're soap operas really. I've so far produced two original graphic novels, *Hairy Mary,* and *Hairy Mary in Fun Fur* [published by Slab O Concrete], although the format of each has been lots of short stories making up a larger narrative. I'm currently developing Hairy Mary as a series of short Flash cartoons.

craig conlan

'With my comic work, I have much more control. I can use whatever font I want for lettering. If the text is overlapping a figure, I can move the character, shrink it or reduce the size/leading of the text. I can add colour, greytones, atmospheric filters or huge sound effects. I do everything on a different layer so that I can change or delete something. I could create a custom font for one character's dialogue.

'At the moment, I'm creating each comic page in Flash. This means I can export it as a vector or a bitmap file, or the artwork could be used to make an animated version of the strip for promotional purposes. I can be wholly responsible for all the graphic design and typography in my comics. This all means much more work for me, of course, but it means that I can be an auteur if I want to. It's just as personal a work as it is with artists who pencil, ink and letter their work the old-fashioned, organic way – although they probably don't have to do any scanning, so I'm suffering more for my art.'

'Recently, I've been doing "paperless" comic pages with my Wacom pen. I can build up layers of sketches as I would have done with layout paper until eventually you have the inked version, and you can delete all the "pencil" layers. It's something I wish to pursue, but it won't replace paper completely for me until I'm directly drawing on screen. Wacom has made inroads already with this type of hardware, but it's not wireless, and it's still very expensive. I'm waiting for the technology to catch up with the hardware I've invented in my head. I'm sure it will soon.'

Right: **Noodles,** *another Conlan tour de force, is very Japanese in flavour.*

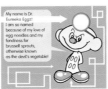

A SHOWCASE OF THE BEST THRILLS IN THE BUSINESS

toon thrills

Ready for action? Tales of adventure have fuelled the comics industry more than any other genre. Dynamic pages and poses make for a high-impact reading experience.

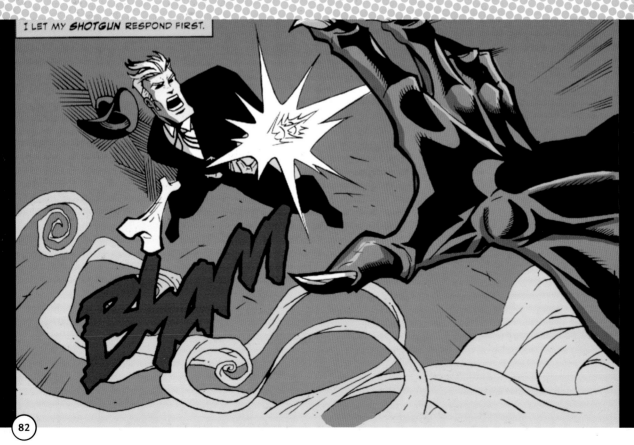

I LET MY *SHOTGUN* RESPOND FIRST.

Left: *A display of physical force is paramount in this powerful panel by Shannon Denton.*

END

Above: *Packed panel arrangements like this one push the story forwards at an almost frenetic pace, helping to quicken the reader's pulse.*

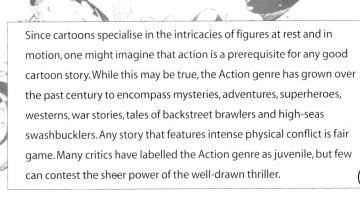

Since cartoons specialise in the intricacies of figures at rest and in motion, one might imagine that action is a prerequisite for any good cartoon story. While this may be true, the Action genre has grown over the past century to encompass mysteries, adventures, superheroes, westerns, war stories, tales of backstreet brawlers and high-seas swashbucklers. Any story that features intense physical conflict is fair game. Many critics have labelled the Action genre as juvenile, but few can contest the sheer power of the well-drawn thriller.

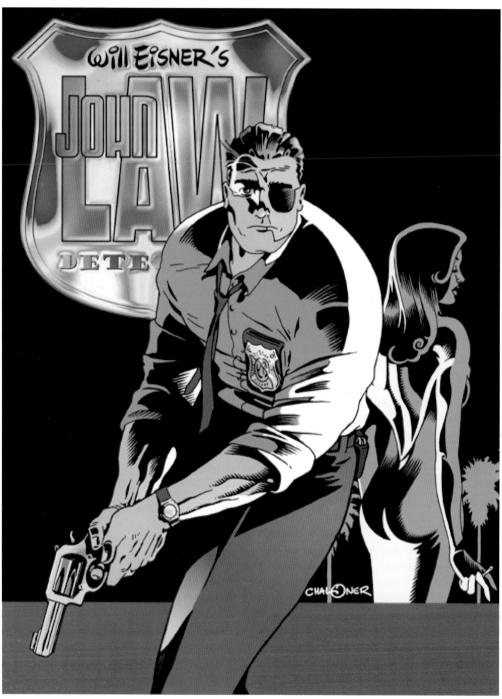

gary chaloner

❝ The computer and the Web have affected my creative process very little.

The hard work is still done on the art board the old-fashioned way. Story is still everything.

Content over form. The computer is just a tool. Damn convenient, though. ❞

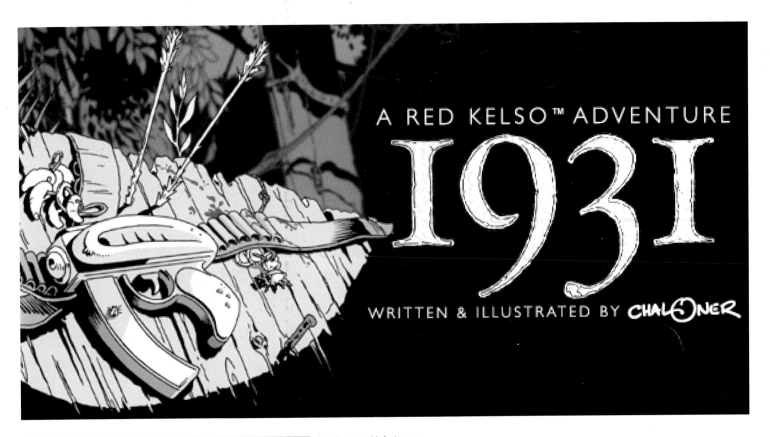

A RED KELSO™ ADVENTURE
1931
WRITTEN & ILLUSTRATED BY CHALONER

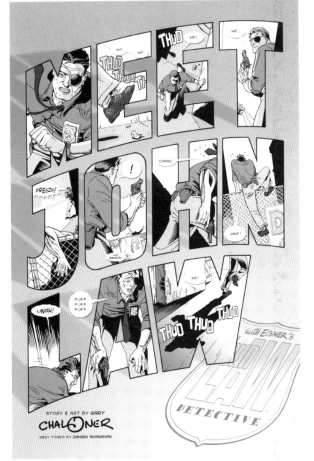

Above and left: *Images from Chaloner's own* Red Kelso *and his 'resurrection' of* John Law, *a character created in 1939 by the legendary Will Eisner.*

'The launching of the *John Law* series by Gary Chaloner represents a very important episode in my career. After all, it is most unusual for a character created so long ago to be given new life in the hands of someone as able as Gary. In all the years of my experience in this field, there have been very few resurrections that succeeded. I eagerly await the experience of witnessing the development of John Law in the world Chaloner's creative mind will build. Go, man, go!'
Will Eisner, July 2001

COUNTRY:
AUSTRALIA

SITE ADDRESSES:
WWW.GARYCHALONER.COM
WWW.MODERNTALES.COM
WWW.OZCOMICS.COM
WWW.ADVENTURESTRIPS.COM

HARDWARE:
MACINTOSH G4, FLATBED SCANNER

SOFTWARE:
ADOBE PHOTOSHOP, FREEHAND, FIREWORKS, DREAMWEAVER

❛ *Essentially, I have one foot firmly planted in print comics and one foot in webcomics. Print is still the more powerful guiding force (i.e., I colour using CMYK colour, and the level of detail is mostly dictated by print). It seems to just be a nice situation that my work lends itself to a certain degree of on-screen legibility.* ❜

jason little

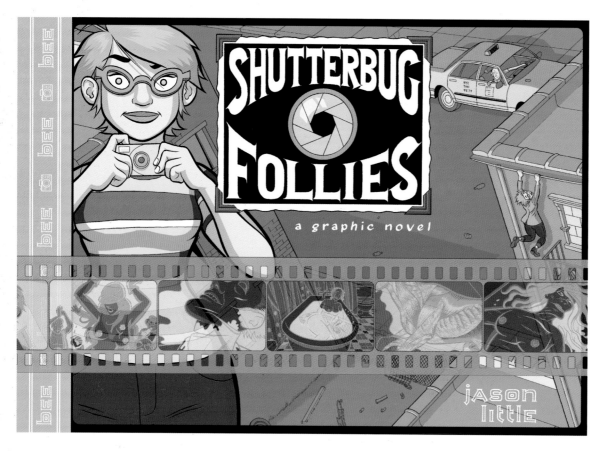

COUNTRY:
US

SITE ADDRESSES:
WWW.BEECOMIX.COM

HARDWARE:
PC, SCANNER, WACOM TABLET

SOFTWARE:
ABOBE PHOTOSHOP, QUARK XPRESS, DREAMWEAVER, MICROSOFT WORD, FONTOGRAPHER

'Having one foot still in print, I am very aware of the difference in resolution between the printed page and the computer screen. I'm hoping that print won't disappear completely until screen resolutions improve to match it.'

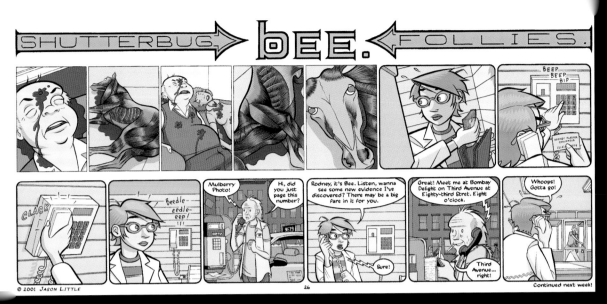

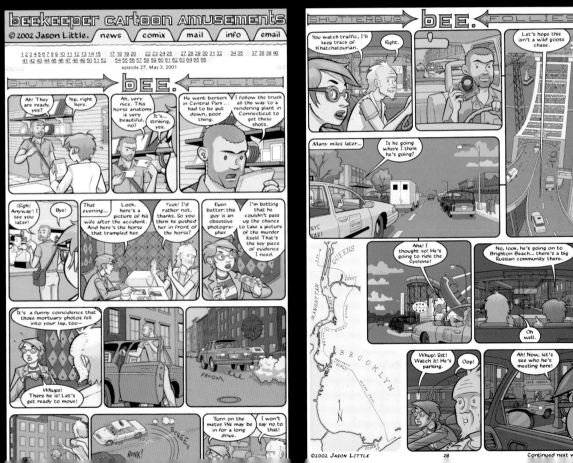

Above: *A suspenseful page from Zabel's mystery series*, Return of the Green Skull.

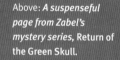

' I profited a great deal from working with Harvey Pekar on his realistic, autobiographical series, American Splendor. *I try to bring some of that sensibility to the mystery comics I've done over the past few years.*

Since becoming a digital artist, I've devoted myself to creating a photographic, 3D style that's outside of the cartooning mainstream. This fits like a glove with my interest in creating realistic comics. '

COUNTRY:
US

SITE ADDRESSES:
WWW.MODERNTALES.COM
HTTP://AMAZINGMONTAGE.TRIPOD.
COM/TRESPASSERS

HARDWARE:
MAC G4 WITH DUAL PROCESSOR,
LARGE-SIZE WACOM TABLET, NON-
DIGITAL CAMERA

SOFTWARE:
CURIOUS LABS POSER,
ADOBE PHOTOSHOP

joe zabel

Right: *Zabel brings his years of experience as a print cartoonist to webcomics in* Rapid Eye Movement *and* Return of the Green Skull.

'As a method of creating comics, digital art is mostly used by cartoonists to enhance or refine the traditional pen-and-ink art styles. The vast potential of digital art is rarely explored. It does have a high degree of penetration in cartoonists' working methods, however, which promises greater developments in the future.

'As a method of distributing comics, webcomics have revolutionized the medium, bringing an explosion of new talent into the field. The quality of webcomics is rather compromised, however, by the difficulty in making it a paying proposition. That's why subscription webcomics services like *Modern Tales* are so important to the future of webcomics.'

 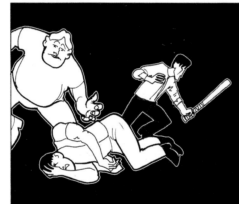 

Above: *Mystery gives way to two-fisted action in Tim Broderick's* Odd Jobs.

tim broderick

‘ *I really enjoy the mystery genre. Not crime comics, but mystery novels. So I wanted to combine my love of mysteries with the comics form.* ’

COUNTRY:
US

SITE ADDRESSES:
HTTP://ODDJOBS.KEENSPACE.COM
WWW.MODERNTALES.COM

HARDWARE:
IMAC, AGFA SCANNER, HP PRINTER

SOFTWARE:
ABOBE PHOTOSHOP,
MACROMEDIA FREEHAND

'The Web was actually what jump-started me after more than a decade's layoff. The kind of story I like to tell, and the way I draw, are just not the dominant comic form right now. The Web provided a way of distributing my work and reaching an audience that, for a long time, I was told just wasn't there. That's turned out to be not true. And finding and keeping that audience has been very fulfilling. Now, if only there was money...

'The second bonus is the ability to publish beyond the constraints of the printed page. There's some terrific examples of the "infinite page" out there, and people are experimenting with animation and other technologies. In my own humble way, I'm taking advantage of the Web's ability to allow an 'infinite' number of pages. It would be pretty expensive to publish a 200-page book for a small audience. Few print publishers would chance it. On the Web, I'm able to produce a novel in the truest sense, without putting my family in the poor house.'

Left: *Broderick's use of black-and-white intensifies the stark violence of the scene.*

dirk tiede

' *I think comics have a really bright future on the Web. It's so disheartening to see the print comics community in the state it's in: ruled primarily by one rarely changing genre that limits the kind of readers who are likely to be brought in. However, on the Web, there's so much more variety. People who couldn't care less about the hot superhero title of the month are tuning in to daily webstrips for a laugh.* '

'While my own stories are probably most likely to appeal to more typical print-comics readers or manga/anime fans, it's so encouraging to see things like Justine Shaw's *Nowhere Girl* or Cat Garza's *Cuentos de la Frontera*. Stuff like that is bound to bring brand-new people to comics.

'To tell the truth, if it hadn't been for the Web and digital tools, I might not have tried doing comics again in the first place. When I first started, I was unsure

COUNTRY:

US

SITE ADDRESSES:

WWW.MODERNTALES.COM

WWW.DYNAMANGA.NET

HARDWARE:

APPLE POWERMAC G4, 35-MM CAMERA

SOFTWARE:

ADOBE PHOTOSHOP, ADOBE ILLUSTRATOR, COREL BRYCE

whether my drawing skills would be up to the task, since I hadn't tried drawing comics in nearly six years. I had been out of college for a year working as a multimedia specialist, so I was far more comfortable working digitally than using natural media at that point. I just decided "what the hell" and took the plunge. Now after working on it for a few years, I've found that having the freedom to infinitely manipulate what I have drawn really takes the pressure off and lets me experiment, since I know I can always fix it later.

'With the Web, I find I'm far more motivated to produce now that I have a specific deadline. Originally, posting on the Web had been more of an afterthought. The idea had been to produce a graphic novel and just put it online until I could get it published. However, I eventually found a small fanbase, and now that I know I have an audience, the payback is far more immediate, since I know that people will be seeing my work almost as soon as I post it.'

Much of Tiede's visual vocabulary, as seen in his Paradigm Shift *and* Tesseract, *derives from the 'rendering' and 'masking' effects of Japanese manga.*

COUNTRY:
US

SITE ADDRESSES:
WWW.METEORCITY.NET
WWW.KOMIKWERKS.COM

HARDWARE:
'PCS I'VE MADE TO FIT MY SPECIFICATIONS.'

SOFTWARE:
ADOBE PHOTOSHOP

94

'The computer and the Web have allowed me to be more hands-on in all aspects of the creation, as well as the marketing process, of making a comic.'

shannon denton

'I like to come up with stories that aren't "kiddie", but that a kid could enjoy as much as an adult.'

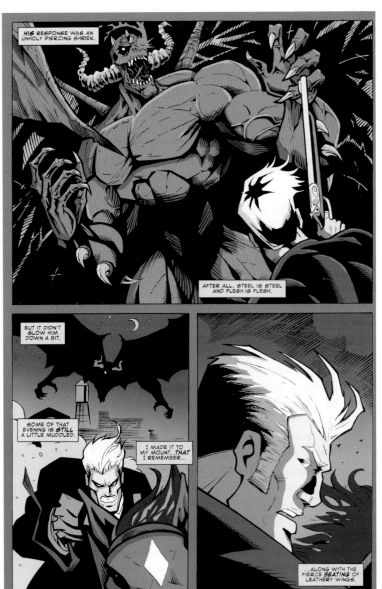

'Right now I see digital media as a great way to reach people outside of the normal scope of print. I think people who buy print comics will continue to do so even if they saw the same work online, as long as the quality of the merchandise remains high. With the Web, there is a much greater reach to the kinds of exposure a project can get.'

'Starting Komikwerks.com with Patrick Coyle [in 2000] I saw as my chance to give back to the comics community. I realized we could just talk about doing this or we could organize an effort among professionals to have their work viewed by many. I've been doing comics for over nine years, having worked for Marvel, DC and everyone else, and I now work full-time as an animation director in LA. I knew my work was professional, but I also knew how many talented people I work with on a daily basis who have expressed interest but had concerns about making a comic for one reason or another. I'm just trying to remove some of those concerns and encourage these talented individuals to pursue their art so the rest of us can enjoy it.'

toon reveries

We each have visions of other worlds, other lives. But how can we share our fantasies with others? With cartoons, it is as simple as drawing our dreams.

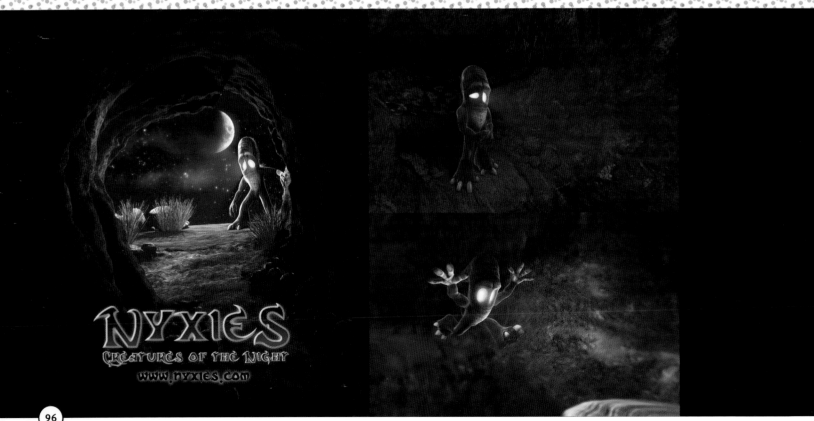

NYXIES
CREATURES OF THE NIGHT
www.nyxies.com

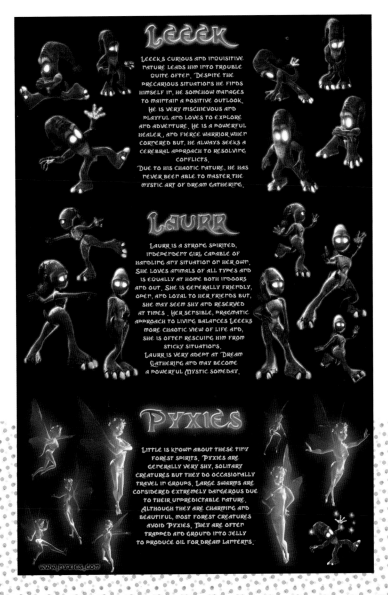

LEEEK

LEEEK'S CURIOUS AND INQUISITIVE NATURE LEADS HIM INTO TROUBLE QUITE OFTEN. DESPITE THE PRECARIOUS SITUATIONS HE FINDS HIMSELF IN, HE SOMEHOW MANAGES TO MAINTAIN A POSITIVE OUTLOOK. HE IS VERY MISCHIEVOUS AND PLAYFUL AND LOVES TO EXPLORE AND ADVENTURE. HE IS A POWERFUL HEALER, AND FIERCE WARRIOR WHEN CORNERED BUT, HE ALWAYS SEEKS A CEREBRAL APPROACH TO RESOLVING CONFLICTS. DUE TO HIS CHAOTIC NATURE, HE HAS NEVER BEEN ABLE TO MASTER THE MYSTIC ART OF DREAM GATHERING.

LAURR

LAURR IS A STRONG SPIRITED, INDEPENDENT GIRL CAPABLE OF HANDLING ANY SITUATION ON HER OWN. SHE LOVES ANIMALS OF ALL TYPES AND IS EQUALLY AT HOME BOTH INDOORS AND OUT. SHE IS GENERALLY FRIENDLY, OPEN, AND LOYAL TO HER FRIENDS BUT, SHE MAY SEEM SHY AND RESERVED AT TIMES. HER SENSIBLE, PRAGMATIC APPROACH TO LIVING BALANCES LEEEKS MORE CHAOTIC VIEW OF LIFE AND, SHE IS OFTEN RESCUING HIM FROM STICKY SITUATIONS. LAURR IS VERY ADEPT AT DREAM GATHERING AND MAY BECOME A POWERFUL MYSTIC SOMEDAY.

PYXIES

LITTLE IS KNOWN ABOUT THESE TINY FOREST SPIRITS. PYXIES ARE GENERALLY VERY SHY, SOLITARY CREATURES BUT THEY DO OCCASIONALLY TRAVEL IN GROUPS. LARGE SWARMS ARE CONSIDERED EXTREMELY DANGEROUS DUE TO THEIR UNPREDICTABLE NATURE. ALTHOUGH THEY ARE CHARMING AND BEAUTIFUL, MOST FOREST CREATURES AVOID PYXIES. THEY ARE OFTEN TRAPPED AND GROUND INTO JELLY TO PRODUCE OIL FOR DREAM LANTERNS.

www.nyxies.com

Above: *Fantasy images from Mike Brown's independent short film,* Nyxies. Right: *Image by Gareth Hinds.*

Fantasy is the most incorrigible of genres because it is patently impossible to pin down the human imagination. All stories are products of fancy, so why do we call only certain stories 'fantasies'? To that, there is no simple answer.

In our myths, legends, fables, fairytales and folktales, we tend the delightful and sometimes devilish garden from which all our modern fictions have grown. As many dreamer-artists have attested, from Homer to Tolkien, this fantasy garden is at once an alluring and an alarming place.

Categories of contemporary fantasy include 'dark' fantasy or supernatural horror, heroic fantasy or sword-and-sorcery, magical realism, urban fantasy, humorous fantasy, historical fantasy, superhero or power fantasy and alternate-universe fantasy. Today there are cartoonists specialising in each of these sub-genres, and their cartoons have given us some of our brightest and most frightful visions.

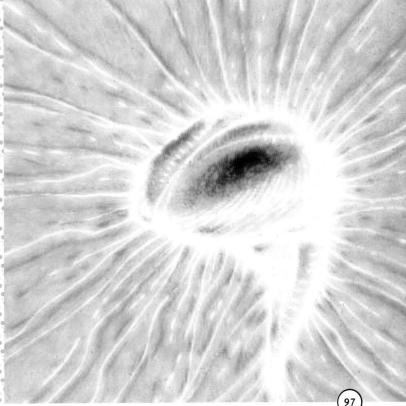

COUNTRY:
CANADA

SITE ADDRESSES:
WWW.MAKESHIFTMIRACLE.COM
WWW.MODERNTALES.COM

HARDWARE:
PENTIUM 4 1.6GHZ, GEFORCE 2TI

SOFTWARE:
ADOBE PHOTOSHOP

jim zubkavich

'The Web levels the playing field in many areas, but just because everyone has the tools, it doesn't mean that everyone can create professional-quality work. It will make it easier for the best people to showcase their work, but classical art and design training will still push people ahead of the pack.'

'The Web has opened up a ton of possibilities for me. Distribution of my work is simple and painless, giving me a lot more time to concentrate on the work itself. I think that the most creative people would love to be in a vacuum, just working on what they love without interference. Doing my work digitally gives me a much greater degree of that, minimising the frustrating little tasks that take away from the creativity.'

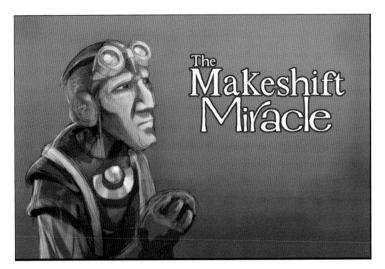

> ❛ The flexibility of digitally colouring my pages allows me a lot more opportunities to experiment with different styles and approaches. I can save multiple versions and try them out until I'm satisfied with a final product. ❜

Above, left, and right: *Beautifully rendered and coloured pages from the surreal fantasy,* The Makeshift Miracle.

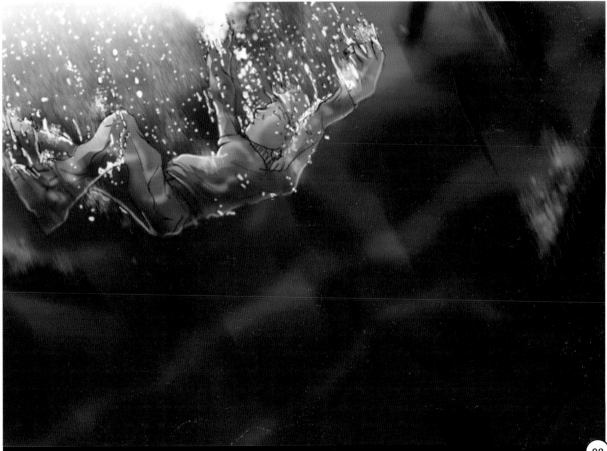

by AP. FURTADO

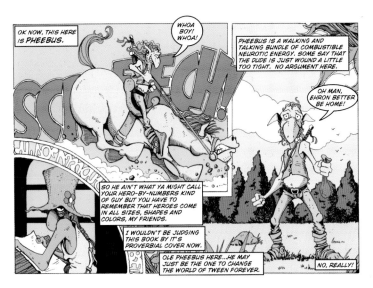

COUNTRY:
US

SITE ADDRESSES:
WWW.BRISTOLTHUGS.COM/TWEEN
WWW.APFURTADO.COM

HARDWARE:
DELL DIMENSION 4400 PENTIUM 4
1.80 GHZ, HP SCANJET 4400C

SOFTWARE:
ADOBE PHOTOSHOP, ABOBE
ILLUSTRATOR

anthony furtado

'I'm probably just another cog in the machinery, but as long as that machine which is digital comics keeps rolling forwards, then any cog is a good cog. My work may stand out from the rest because it's different. Maybe not so much original, but more of a throwback to the days of Underground comix and the early 70s. I'm not striving to re-invent the digital comics medium. I'm just trying to put out an entertaining strip both visually and storywise. It has to be entertaining for me first. Seems to be working so far.'

'I think the world of digital comics has truly begun to take shape. There've been a few roses among the thorns in the past, but for the most part digital comics were thought of as the wasteland for folks who couldn't make it in the print comics world. Roses are beginning to bloom in the digital comics world now.'

Left: *Furtado's quirky fantasy,* Tween, *is a bright new light in the vast realm of online comics.*

indigo kelleigh

❛ *I think my work stands out as one of the few real high-fantasy, long-form comics out there. I'm telling a long story; here it's not just a bunch of characters in various adventures, it's one long adventure.* ❜

'I wouldn't be doing *Circle Weave* right now if I couldn't publish it as cheaply as I do online. The Web has allowed me to experiment with doing comics in full colour, which has changed my technical process as well, adding another step to drawing the comic. Drawing the comic digitally has also created some new issues for me, namely that I no longer have original artwork lying around. I can go back and change things that were messed up or forgotten, or that just didn't work quite right the first time. I've gotten too used to the tablet, though, and I start to become afraid of drawing the traditional way – there's no undo, and the tools are messier.'

'Digital entertainment, or specifically online digital entertainment, is still in its infancy primarily because nobody's proven that there's any money in it. The only type of online digital entertainment that's proven itself is video games, and, well, porn, but that's a whole other ball of wax.'

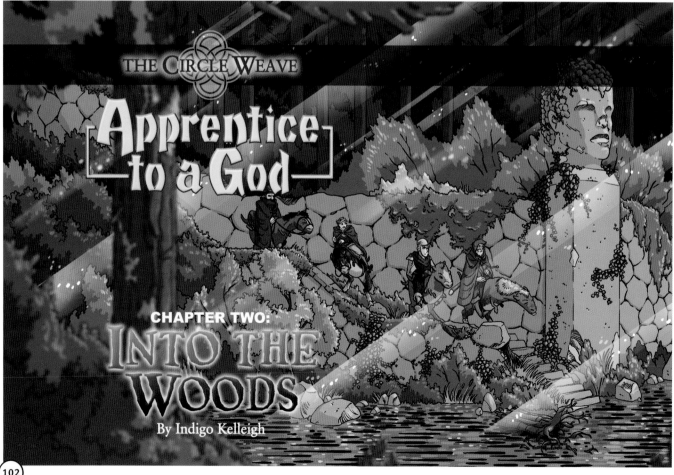

COUNTRY:
US

SITE ADDRESSES:
WWW.CIRCLEWEAVE.COM
WWW.MODERNTALES.COM
WWW.XENITE.ORG
WWW.KOMIKWERKS.COM

HARDWARE:
MACINTOSH G4 DUAL 533MHZ,
WACOM INTUOS 6X8 DRAWING
TABLET

SOFTWARE:
ADOBE PHOTOSHOP 6, ADOBE
ILLUSTRATOR, FONTOGRAPHER,
IMAGEREADY

6 *When writing* The Circle Weave, *I have a very rough outline of the story in place and I refine it in sections. I've got the current chapter roughed out in a page-by-page text format. Then, when it comes to doing each page, I'll sit and do the script and rough layouts at the same time. It makes it a bit more organic, as they are developed in tandem. I don't work from an existing script or anything; I do it all together.* 9

'*Abby's Menagerie is a pretty big story with an intricate plot that is going to take several years for us to tell.*'

jenni & barry gregory

'The computer has always been an integral part of the way we make comics. In early 2000, we decided to concentrate our publishing efforts on the Web, but initially there really weren't a lot of changes in the way we produced work for the Web as opposed to print. At first, we did add some limited animation to our stories – mostly just timing the panels and the balloons to load in the order that they should be read, but in a relatively short period of time Barry and I both became convinced that this was a bad idea. Rather than enhancing the reading experience, we came to believe that the animations and the movement were nothing more than a distraction. Comics require the reader to

COUNTRY:
US

SITE ADDRESS:
WWW.ABBYSMENAGERIE.COM

HARDWARE:
PC, GRAPHICS TABLET, FLATBED
SCANNER, DIGITAL CAMERA

SOFTWARE:
MACROMEDIA FLASH, ADOBE
PHOTOSHOP, MACROMEDIA
FIREWORKS, COREL DRAW

participate in the storytelling experience. They're a lot more like books in that they require reader participation to make the story come to life. You can't just sit back and let them do all the work. The panels are just little snippets of action. The reader's imagination fills in the gaps. And if all the pistons are firing, the reader forgets that he's looking at static images. In the mind's eye, these static images are actually flowing across the page and the action continues past the panel gutters. But if the figures actually ARE moving across a static panel or balloons, and sound effects are popping in sequential order, then the reader is never fully engaged, never fully participates in the storytelling process. The overall effect is greatly lessened.'

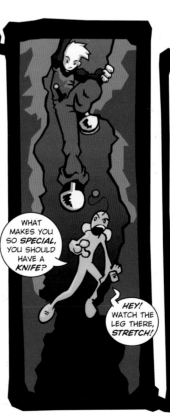

US

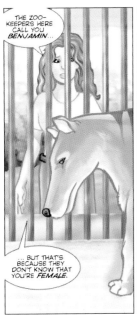
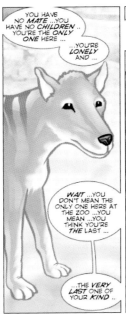
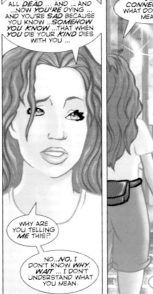
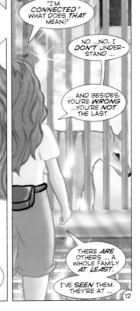

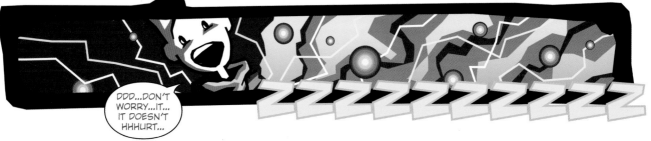

106

jeff crowther

'The digital comics medium is very fun and exciting to be a part of right now. Everything seems new and bold, since, actually, digital comics are in their infancy. One of the great things about digital comics is the true diversity of styles and subject matter you can find on the Web that you just can't get in comics or the newspapers. Digital comics, and especially those appearing on the Web, refuse to simply be another place to tell stories about super-heroes or to run four-panel gag strips. People are telling a wide variety of stories and breaking conventional concepts of storytelling by exploring the potential of the medium.'

❛ *I've learned to format comic pages for the screen rather than the printed page. Being able to use colour without having to worry about costs is incredibly liberating as far as creativity is concerned. Also, working digitally is great because no change you make to your artwork has to be permanent. You can always undo and try again. This allows for a lot of experimentation with colours and shapes, and really just about anything.* ❜

COUNTRY:
US

SITE ADDRESSES:
WWW.MODERNTALES.COM
WWW.ODDITYCOMICS.COM

HARDWARE:
POWER MAC G3, CANON SCANNER

SOFTWARE:
ADOBE ILLUSTRATOR,
ADOBE PHOTOSHOP,
MACROMEDIA DREAMWEAVER

Above: *A still from Taylor's 3D animated short film,* Rustboy. *Taylor chose to forego the use of high-end 3D software to see how professional a result he could achieve 'on a shoestring budget and a bit of imagination'.*

Right: *Character shots of Taylor's wide-eyed title character, who was brought electrically to life in Frankenstein fashion.*

brian taylor

COUNTRY:
UK

SITE ADDRESSES:
WWW.RUSTBOY.COM

HARDWARE:
POWERPC G4

SOFTWARE:
INFINI-D, CARRARA,
ADOBE PHOTOSHOP,
PREMIERE

'I started playing around with animation as soon as I got into computers in general (it's been about ten years now), but *Rustboy* is my first serious stab at animation.

'I tend to do everything 'by hand' from scratch rather than using effects and plug-ins which are built into the 3D software. I always have a good idea of the look or effect I'm after, and figure out my own ways of achieving that look rather than getting into the latest software which does a lot of it for you.'

' I think that the digital realm
makes it possible for people who
have the talent but maybe didn't
have the means to create traditional
animation. I think we'll see a lot
more independent animated movies
surfacing in the future. '

chris bailey

‘ *If I were to guess what makes my work stand out, it might be how I apply my Disney animation experience to realistic 3-D effects. I try to go for a stylized reality that is more appealing than true*

COUNTRY:
US

SITE ADDRESSES:
WWW.MAJORDAMAGE.ORG

HARDWARE:
HP VISUALIZE WORKSTATION,
POWER MAC 8500, G4

SOFTWARE:
MAYA, SHAKE, ADOBE
PHOTOSHOP, ADOBE
ILLUSTRATOR, PREMIERE

Left: *More stills from Major Damage. Bailey's other work includes animation and direction for Disney Feature Animation and Don Bluth Studios.*

reality. When it comes down to between reality and appeal, I'll take appeal every time. Many CG animators without traditional training are afraid to exaggerate motion for fear of being "too cartoony". I have no such fear! **'**

'Shortly after leaving Disney, when I finished my assignment on *Hercules*, I came up with *Major Damage*. I wrote and registered a one-page movie outline and drew out the concept as an eight-page comics story just for the fun of it. I liked it so much that I wanted to direct a short animation of the characters. It wasn't meant to be a pitch piece for a film or TV series, but I knew it could work as one if chose to go that way. So I adapted the comic-book story into a storyboard that would introduce Major Damage, a genetically engineered, monster-fighting superhero, and Melvin, the boy who is obsessed with him.

'The storyboard sat unproduced in my studio for some time until a chance meeting at an animation panel with independent film producer, Kellie-Bea Cooper. She offered to help me assemble a crew and find our hardware and software sponsors in HP, Alias and Nothing Real. Doug Cooper, the CG

Supervisor for *Major Damage*, created an online "file depot", where our crew could exchange files and review each other's work. Over the next two years, we worked in between the cracks of our day jobs to finish the film. Crew members would come and go, and then sometimes come back. Slowly but surely we made progress until we eventually reached our goal.

'When animation was complete, Scott Mosier – a friend of mine who produced the *Clerks* cartoon series I directed – introduced me to Gary Rizzo, a sound mixer who works up at Skywalker Ranch. Gary liked *Damage* and agreed to do the sound design and mix.'

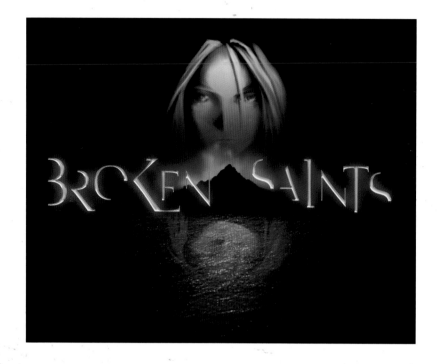

NAMES:
BROOKE BURGESS
IAN KIRBY
ANDREW WEST

COUNTRY:
CANADA

SITE ADDRESSES:
WWW.BROKENSAINTS.COM
WWW.IWANTMYFLASHTV.COM
WWW.MP4.COM

HARDWARE:
PC, WACOM TABLET

SOFTWARE:
COREL PAINTER, ADOBE PHOTOSHOP,
TOONBOOM STUDIO, MACROMEDIA
FLASH, ADOBE ILLUSTRATOR, ADOBE
STREAMLINE, SOUNDFORGE,
FLASHANTS.COM, FTP VOYAGER,
MICROSOFT WORD

broken saints

'Our collaboration is a classic case of self-taught creators being unaware of a medium's limitations. After spending three years in the trenches at a prestigious videogame company, I was eager to branch off and tell my own stories. Rather than attempt to do something in a traditional way (paper comics, watered-down teleplays, etc.), the idea was to use this new medium with a built-in global audience to embark on a serial adventure. The Internet allows for great freedom of expression, and the chance to operate with complete control over the work was intriguing.

'In the summer of 2000, my friendship with a self-taught anime illustrator (Andrew West) led to talk of doing some form of online comic. Andrew introduced me to Ian Kirby, who had already mastered countless software applications and was tinkering with Flash. After watching a painful amount of Flash cartoons, it seemed clear that most creators were using the tools for the lowest common denominators of entertainment: violence and toilet humour. Either that, or they were trying to re-create mediums that already existed, but on a smaller scale: the Flash version of movies, of television or of traditional cartoons.'
Brooke Burgess

WHAT WOULD YOU GIVE

TO KNOW THE TRUTH?

'Broken Saints *stands out because it combines the three things that Web users are most comfortable with – pictures, music and text – and fuses them together in a unique form of narrative. It takes the best aspects from the world of "graphic literature" (exposed thought and character subtext) and the cinematic world (dynamic cameras and engaging effects) to make something new: "Cinematic Literature".* '

Brooke Burgess

Above and right:
*Images from the anime-
inspired, multiple
award-winning Flash film,
Broken Saints.*

CHAPTER FOUR

A SHOWCASE OF THE BEST SCI-FI IN THE BUSINESS

toon travels

From beyond the outer planets to the limits of time itself, the science-fiction genre asks the eternal question 'What if...?' and suggests all manner of plausible possibilities.

Left: *Strip from Shaenon K Garrity's speculative humour comic,* Narbonic.

Right: *Images from* CyberCity CabKiller, *by Barrett Lombardo and Andy Crestodina.*

Far right: *Page from* It's Walky *by David Willis.*

Science fiction, also called speculative fiction or SF, stems from the ancient traditions of satire and utopian literature. The conflict between empiricism and fantasy – science and imagination, reason and emotion – drives the genre, and the full spectrum of SF includes a multitude of sub-genres.

Historically, SF as it applies to cartooning has lagged behind its prose and movie counterparts. With the birth of the 'pulp' magazines in America with Hugo Gernsback's *Modern Electrics* in 1910, the SF genre expanded its audience and its scope, but was widely labelled 'escapist trash' and 'stories for boys', and SF cartoons received a similar distinction. The 1920s brought the popular space heroes Flash Gordon and Buck Rogers to the newspaper comics page. However, throughout the next four decades, cartoonists, in America at least (see Chapter One for a brief discussion of SF's role in Japan and Europe), rarely ventured beyond the comfortable 'sci-fi' trappings of 'space opera' and 'space western', largely ignoring the innovations of SF's prose vanguard, which included Asimov, Simek and Bradbury, and later Vonnegut, Silverberg and Zelazny. In the early 1950s, William Gaines's EC Comics published some better-than-average SF stories,

and SF motifs were often employed, sometimes admirably, in the soon-to-be-dominant superhero comics, but SF as a unique 'genre of ideas' was not well represented in American comics and animation until the 1970s.

When George Lucas released *Star Wars* in 1977, SF lunged forwards in popular acceptance and appeal. That same year, Ralph Bakshi's *Wizards* premiered, setting a new standard in SF animation, followed in 1982 by Don Bluth's *The Secret of NIMH* (based on Robert C. O'Brien's young-adult novel about mutated lab rats). The 1980s and 1990s brought digital technology to the forefront of popular culture, and SF writers and artists invented new brands of speculation, including 'cyberpunk' and 'hard SF', story concepts rooted in the principles and applications of current scientific theory.

Some recent standard bearers in SF animation are Don Bluth's *Titan AE* (2000) and Disney's *Atlantis* (2001) and *Treasure Planet* (2002). Truly exploratory comics such as Christian Gossett's *The Red Star* and Patrick Farley's online *Delta Thrives* are helping to give sequential art a more reputable space in the expanding cosmos of science fiction.

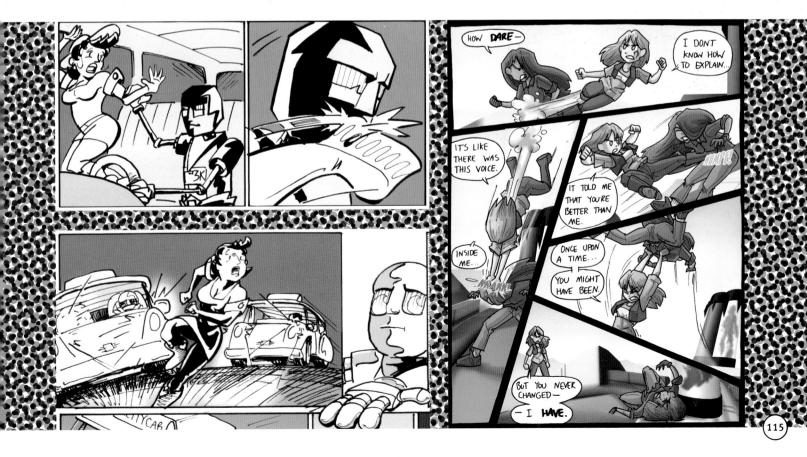

Conley 'tooncasts' his Astounding Space Thrills and BLOOP.*tv to thousands of websites daily. His lively storytelling style and his well-reasoned business model have inspired many other cartoonists to take their work online.

Right: *The title image from Conley's* Astounding Space Thrills, *one of the longest-running and most accessible strips on the Web (and now also available in print).*

' *I don't think of my work in terms of other cartoonists. I simply try to produce the most entertaining and fun stories I can, in the most universal formats I can think of. The only thing I can do is produce every day – whether it be advances in the COMICON.com Web community, a new* Astounding Space Thrills *daily comic strip, a page of the* AST *comic book or the next animated webisode of BLOOP.tv.* '

COUNTRY:
US

SITE ADDRESSES:
WWW.ASTOUNDINGSPACETHRILLS.COM
WWW.BLOOP.TV
WWW.COMICON.COM
WWW.ADVENTURESTRIPS.COM
WWW.STEVECONLEY.COM

HARDWARE:
APPLE MACINTOSH G3 AND APPLE IBOOK

SOFTWARE:
ADOBE PHOTOSHOP,
ADOBE IMAGEREADY, MACROMEDIA
FREEHAND, BBEDIT, MACROMEDIA
DREAMWEAVER, MACROMEDIA FLASH

steve conley

'I've been using Macs for more than 16 years and creating comics with them for nearly that long. I can't imagine working without computers. I use the technology to draw, ink, letter, colour and design my work at every stage. I use the Web for distribution and research. It's become such a part of me that even when I'm not using a computer, I think "undo" from time to time when working in traditional media. That said, I still prefer to outline, write and sketch my comics as far away from computers as possible – usually outside my studio, in a coffee shop, or diner. Anyplace I can get good coffee.'

Left and right: *All-digital panels from Parker's pioneering* Argon Zark!, *arguably the world's first online comic.*

charley parker

' *The fact that I do the technical side myself allows me to make the interactive and Web design elements integral to the nature of the strip. Unlike a lot of transplanted print comics,* Argon Zark! *is in its natural space on the Web.* '

COUNTRY:
US

SITE ADDRESS:
WWW.ZARK.COM

HARDWARE:
POWER MAC G4, WACOM INTUOS TABLET

SOFTWARE:
COREL PAINTER, ADOBE PHOTOSHOP, KAI'S POWER TOOLS, BOXTOP GIFMATION, MACROMEDIA FLASH, MACROMEDIA FIREWORKS, COREL BRYCE, BBEDIT, ADOBE GOLIVE

'I write, draw, ink, colour and letter the story myself, and I also do all of the HTML, dHTML, JavaScript, GIF animation and Flash animation. As a result, I'm at much more liberty to experiment than most creators who specialize in one aspect or who must work with a team.

'I get some credit as an originator. As far as I can determine, I was the first to put an online comic on the Web (*Argon Zark!* debuted in June 1995). I was probably also the first to create a comic designed specifically for the Web (horizontal format, HTML links between pages, unprintable RGB colours, story focused on the Internet itself, etc.) and one of the first to draw my comics entirely in image-editing software with a Wacom tablet.

'I was also early to use hypertext to provide interactive features and an "expanded" storyline, in which clicking on the images would take the reader to a second or third level of pages designed to deepen and elaborate on the story.

'I was one of the earliest to use image-editing software and filters to create comics images that would have been impossible (or impractical) in traditional illustration.

'When I was first introduced to computer graphics and the Internet in 1994, I immediately got the notion that the Web would be a great place to do a comic book. I went looking for something that I could use as an example or guide and couldn't find anything. There were comics on the Web at that time, but they were mostly scanned copies of existing comic books and funnies in newspaper-strip format. So I just dove in and made it up as I went along.'

'First and foremost, the computer has allowed me to consider colour. With a story that would never interest a major publisher and no trust fund in sight, if *Dicebox* had been printed on paper, it would have been black and white and, I believe, would have suffered for it. Not that I don't love black-and-white comics, but I think of the colour as a major character of this story.

'Nearly as important, the computer provides the flexibility of simply telling a story online. The best stuff on the Internet is usually done by people after their day jobs, so the Web audience has quickly developed an odd patience in seeing something play out, a panel a day, a page a week, etc. I had already witnessed this with works such as Jason Little's *Bee*, and Christopher Baldwin's *Bruno*.

'So, instead of needing to complete an issue and have it printed before you can mark progress, it happens in increments. This not only frees me from the need to create a grabbing, stand-alone issue, it also allows me not to be concerned with filling a printer's spread or exceeding a page count. I can concentrate on what the chapter or story as a whole needs.'

jenn manley lee

COUNTRY:
US

SITE ADDRESS:
WWW.JENNWORKS.COM

HARDWARE:
APPLE IBOOK, WACOM INTUOS TABLET
AND EPSON PERFECTION SCANNER

SOFTWARE:
ADOBE PHOTOSHOP, PROCREATE
PAINTER, ADOBE ILLUSTRATOR, COREL
VECTOR EFFECTS, MACROMEDIA
FONTOGRAPHER

Right: *Dicebox draws its narrative power from the interaction of complex characters rather than from exaggerated physical combat and flashy technical effects common to many SF comics.*

'Dicebox is "futuristic fiction". I make the distinction of "futuristic fiction" as a sort of sub-genre of science fiction, as I am not interested in spotlighting the technology per se, though I am working to develop a convincing premise for it – along with the much more important (to me) social, class and government politics. '

COUNTRY:
US

SITE ADDRESS:
WWW.THEREDSTAR.COM

HARDWARE:
DELL DIMENSION XPS D300,
UMAX POWERLOOK II SCANNER,
MACINTOSH G3, HOMEMADE
UPGRADE

SOFTWARE:
ADOBE PHOTOSHOP, ADOBE
ILLUSTRATOR, QUARK XPRESS,
LIGHTWAVE, 3D STUDIO MAX,
COREL BRYCE

christian gossett

'My own digital era began when I was hired by Activision, Inc. to do character design, which evolved into a job writing dialogue for the animated sequences, which evolved into a gig directing those same sequences. Directing gave me a burning desire to dive fully into the modern movement of bringing digital innovation to illustration. I realized that 3D artwork could be transformed into a tool for comics storytelling. My thought was, since my main strength was illustrating the human figure in action, that I would draw the characters and with these drawings populate a world that was made up mainly of 3D sets. I immediately began searching for other like-minded people who must have been struck by the same idea. It wasn't long before a friend and colleague, Junki Saita, showed me Kia Asamiya's collection of *Dark Angel* covers. The book had pencil line drawings of Asamiya's characters integrated wonderfully into 3D backgrounds. Even though

there were no complete story sequences, the power that was evoked in these single-image, digital character studies proved to me that a new form of visual storytelling was being born. I set my life on target to become one of these pioneers. A story that I'd conceived while living in Berkeley would be the perfect testing ground, a sci-fi fantasy about a group of heroes trying to free their nation from a totalitarian regime. I called the story *The Red Star*.

'I knew the first thing I needed was allies in this fight, so I assembled Team Red Star. The business team consists of dear friends from high school who threw themselves fully into the cause of what quickly evolved from my personal project into our collective vision. The visual team consisted of myself, Jon Moberly on models and Allen Coulter doing the finished renders and using Photoshop to integrate my character drawings into the 3D environments. Just before we went into production, we hired an artist who goes by the nom de guerre "Snakebite", whose sensibility really put the finishing touch on the work. He is a master digital painter and has become my primary collaborator. We began publishing in June 2000 to great acclaim among comics, animation and videogame professionals.'

THE RED STAR

'*What I strive for in my work is vast scale and authentic emotion in the faces of the characters. My strengths in this area derive from a lifelong love of cinema. My father was a professional actor, so I've always had an acute longing to bring an actor's sense of character to my drawings.*'

An early career highlight for Gossett was designing the double lightsabre wielded by Darth Maul in George Lucas's Star Wars: The Phantom Menace.

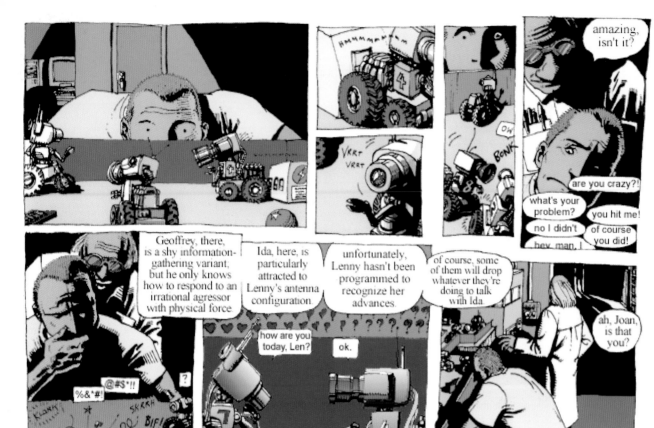

gareth hinds

'The Web gives me total control over the final quality of my print books by allowing me to do my own pre-press. It also gives me another large toolbox to use in creating work, although for the most part I continue to use traditional materials predominantly.

　'The Web gives me the freedom to make any of my work instantly accessible to the public. I can make an experimental, risky webcomic and not worry about whether enough people will like it to cover the "publishing" costs. I can point illustration clients to my portfolio online. I can also do things technically with a webcomic that I can't do in print, such as hyperlinking, changing page formats, animating and so on. The Web also allows me to be a retailer for my own work, again without risking any substantial amount of money to do so. Since most people don't live near a store that carries my work, this is a huge boon.'

COUNTRY:
US

SITE ADDRESS:
WWW.THECOMIC.COM

HARDWARE:
PC, 8X12 AND 12X18 SCANNERS, LASER AND PHOTO INKJET PRINTERS, 12X12 WACOM TABLET

SOFTWARE:
ADOBE PHOTOSHOP

CHAPTER FIVE

A SHOWCASE OF THE BEST CHARACTERS IN THE BUSINESS

toon personas

Like the great novelists and dramatists, cartoonists have examined in their art the intricate inner workings of human relationships to help us define who we truly are.

Left: *Panel from Ethan Persoff's enigmatic digital comic,* Teddy.

Right: *The webcomic* Near Life Experience *is, according to its creator, Lea Hernandez, 'not quite true and not quite fiction'.*

Though still branded as 'low art' by many naysayers, cartoons and the characters who populate them can possess as much emotional depth and intellectual complexity as canonical works of prose literature and stage drama. To prove this point, Art Spiegelman's two *Maus* graphic novels, Chris Ware's *Jimmy Corrigan: The Smartest Kid on Earth*, Joe Sacco's *Safe Area Gorazde* and Keiji Nakazawa's *Barefoot Gen* stand as just a few superb examples of comics that push beyond the limits of melodrama to reveal genuine human truth.

Many digital cartoonists such as those featured in this showcase have similar aims and ambitions, and their works include fictions, autobiographies, biographies and histories, among other genres. If one thread has emerged from so many disparate works, then it might be that digital cartoonists often synthesize real and imaginary experiences, settings and characters to create cohesive narratives of clarity and substance. In these instances, the artist gives the reader something that is greater than the facts yet can also be more grounded than so-called 'escapist' fantasy.

john allison

'Working on the computer has completely changed the way I work. I began drawing in pen and ink, just using the computer to colour; today I rely wholly on the computer – there is no way I could reproduce it by hand. If anything, the Web introduces a greater element of care, because your past work is always available to a new reader.'

COUNTRY:

UK

SITE ADDRESSES:

WWW.SCARYGROUND.COM

WWW.BOBBINS.ORG

HARDWARE:

APPLE IBOOK, WACOM GRAPHIRE TABLET

SOFTWARE:

ADOBE ILLUSTRATOR

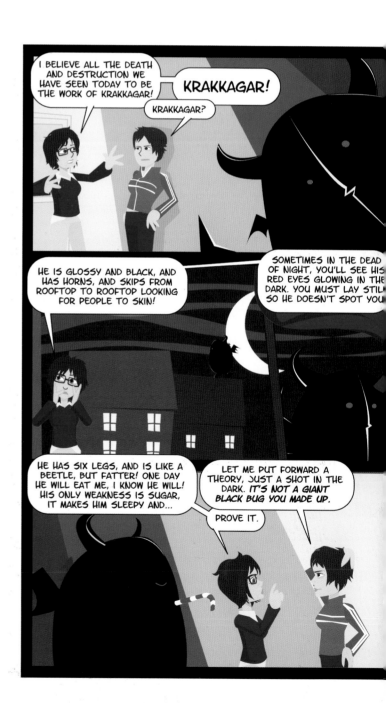

'_Digital comics have opened up a field that was closed to all but the well-off amateur. Instead of saving up for months to put out a small-press comic that would surely make a loss, young creators can expose their work to waiting eyes. If it is good enough, it will find its audience._'

gene yang

COUNTRY:

US

SITE ADDRESSES:

WWW.MODERNTALES.COM

WWW.HUMBLECOMICS.COM

WWW.SMALLSTORIESONLINE.COM

HARDWARE:

MAC POWERBASE 180, IMAC

SOFTWARE:

ADOBE PHOTOSHOP

Above: *Exploring the realm of myth in two pages from Gene Yang's The Monkey King.*

> *Digital media empowers people to be creators. Traditional media had a number of financial and skills barriers that have been torn down by your average $2000 home computer system.*

'The computer lets me pretend to be a better artist than I actually am. If I'm unsatisfied with a particular brush stroke, Photoshop lets me redo it an infinite number of times without caking up little mounds of White-out. And sometime in the near future, when I've gathered enough courage, I plan to experiment with computer colouring. I've been told by other artists that it's the best thing since double-stuffed Oreos.

'I believe that whatever makes an artist unique as an individual – his personality, his value system, his vision of the world – also makes that artist's work unique. I am a male, Roman Catholic, Chinese-American, high-school teacher who loves his wife, enjoys watching cartoons and has a history of sinus problems. I hope all of that shows through in my work.'
Gene Yang

Right: *Life stories and a sense of cultural heritage are at the heart of Gene Yang's work.*

COUNTRY:
US

SITE ADDRESSES:
WWW.NOWHEREGIRL.COM
HTTP://NOWHEREGIRL.WARPED.COM
WWW.JITTERBUG.COM/CLOWN/

HARDWARE:
SELF-BUILT PENTIUM III 500MHZ,
LAPTOP, SCANNER, WACOM TABLET

SOFTWARE:
ADOBE PHOTOSHOP, FRACTAL DESIGN
PAINTER 4, ALLAIRE HOMESITE,
NOTEPAD, WORDPAD

justine shaw

' I like stories about real, messed-up people who try to do right, but often come out causing harm to themselves or others. '

'What's great about the Web right now, it strikes me, is how different it all is. It's like the early days of MTV, before there were millions of dollars in it and every "creative" decision was made by marketing groups. In the beginning, there were just people floundering around, making really weird, kooky stuff that pushed the boundaries of what was considered television. Digital comics seem to have some similar energy to that right now – there's little money in it, and hence little corporate involvement. It's a medium where you're actually reading what people want to write.'

'The computer and the Web allow me to reach people to a degree I never thought I could. Also, for a control freak like myself, it puts nearly everything I need to do a comic within my own power: the only limitation on what I can do is the time I have to do it in. I don't have to rely on other people for almost anything; it's very liberating!'

❛ *My diary comic has spawned numerous imitators. I've sort of created a whole new genre, or a movement. I hadn't meant to, but that's what's happening. Every week I hear from another new cartoonist who was inspired to start a daily diary strip. I was just trying to make sense of what it means to be a human being and to be alive. The daily strip format is the most effective way to express human existence with all its foibles, joys, troubles, ups and downs, and ins and outs – its repetitions and its surprises.* ❜

COUNTRY:
US

SITE ADDRESSES:
WWW.MODERNTALES.COM
WWW.AMERICANELF.COM

HARDWARE:
IMAC

SOFTWARE:
ADOBE PHOTOSHOP

james kochalka

'The main thing the Web has done is increase my level of excitement. There's a much faster and more direct connection between myself and the reader. Within minutes of drawing the strip, it's up on the Web, available for all to see. It just makes the whole experience more thrilling. I can post the strip while the glow of the creative experience is still warm within me. When I draw graphic novels for the print medium, it can take up to a year or two between the completion of the work and its publication. By the time a book sees print, it's almost dead for me already.

'I think that culture is splintering into smaller factions and groups. We don't have to bend our content to appeal to the masses because the Internet allows us easy access to like-minded individuals around the globe. The percentage of the population interested in a comic about a frog with a boner may be quite small, but the Internet allows anyone anywhere access to it. Any bizarre item can find its niche audience.'

Above right: *An amiably agoraphobic entry from Kochalka's groundbreaking online diary strip,* American Elf.

Right: **Fancy Froglin,** *one of Kochalka's most recognisable characters, might be called 'the poster frog' for cartoons on the Web: fresh and fearless and free.*

JOINING AMY IN THE TUB

Let's pretend I climbed the wall of the Playboy Mansion and I sneak in the tub with one of the girls

And she continues to read her book?

JULY 26, 2002

YESTERDAY

I haven't been outside all day

Don't worry. It sucks out there.

TODAY

it doesn't look SO bad

JUNE 13, 2002

I am wearing little pants to hide my genitals.

It is the law!

They are very tight.

It feels funny...

My goodness! I've grown a boner!

I LIKE these pants!

Now I will go for a walk

...to show all my friends the boner I have!

small stories

Why wasn't I ever this reflective and focused(and if I was, why couldn't I express myself--why couldn't I put it into words?) And why didn't I read this at the time? Most importantly, why didn't I get to know this person better?? While my nose was buried in Spider-Man's marital problems and Piers Anthony's horse-sex fetish, real life, real people were passing me by.

What a fool I was.

SELF-LOATHING
SHATTERED DREAMS
CRUSHES
MORE REGRETS
BAD DECISION

THE SOUND
REGRETS
SHAME
SELF-PITY
LOST HOPES

The Sound (c) Derek Kirk 2002.

COUNTRY:
US

SITE ADDRESSES:
WWW.SMALLSTORIESONLINE.COM

HARDWARE:
HP PAVILION PC

SOFTWARE:
WORDPAD, ADOBE PHOTOSHOP

Above: *Two protagonists from Kirk's expansive, character-driven comic,* Small Stories.

Left and above right: *Images illustrating the range of Kirk's comics work, from the dramatic to the humorous.*

derek kirk (ji-hoon gim)

Same Difference (c) Derek Kirk 2002.

Emo Rock Hyung (c) Derek Kirk 2002. Indy Rock Pete (c) R. Stevens 2002.

'The Web really enhances the readers' presence as a story is being slowly unfolded. It connects me to them in a way that's much more intimate than ever before. Since I get feedback and encouragement every single day (as opposed to stretches of two months or more in print comics), it helps me to maintain enthusiasm, focus and perseverance through the duration of a story. Because I have an extremely short attention span, this is more important than it may seem. Another rewarding thing about the Web is that I'm reaching people I would never have, had I remained exclusive to print. Namely, the "average" person who would never walk into a comic-book store.'

I'm an Asian American telling stories starring realistic, three-dimensional, Asian-American characters. As far as I can tell, you don't really see that in ANY visual storytelling medium in America, and nary a one in American comics.

tracy a white

'The first comics I made were for Netscape 1.0 when the average modem speed was 14k. That meant that I wanted to keep my graphics as simple and small as possible to prevent readers from having to wait to see the comic – that's actually why *Traced* is in black and white with occasional accent colours. Originally, I chose to make them as 2-bit images because colour would have made the download time too long. I also realized early on that I didn't want to draw comics by hand and scan them in – it seemed much easier to just draw them straight on the computer. I was lucky that until then I'd only been a reader of comics and therefore had no preconceptions of how I should or shouldn't draw them. Finally, I wanted to be sure that the online comics were unique. I always take into account how things on a computer are different from being on any other medium.'

COUNTRY:
US

SITE ADDRESSES:
WWW.TRACED.COM
WWW.OXYGEN.COM
WWW.GURL.COM

HARDWARE:
MAC G3
WACOM TABLET

SOFTWARE:
PROCREATE PAINTER, ADOBE
IMAGEREADY, BBEDIT,
COMMOTION, AVID

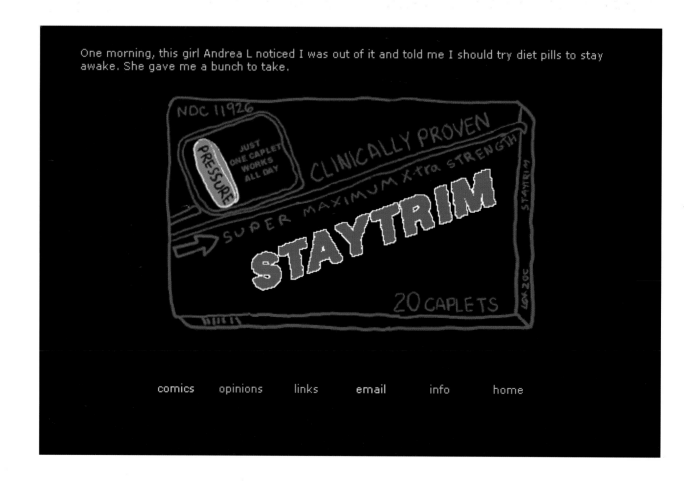

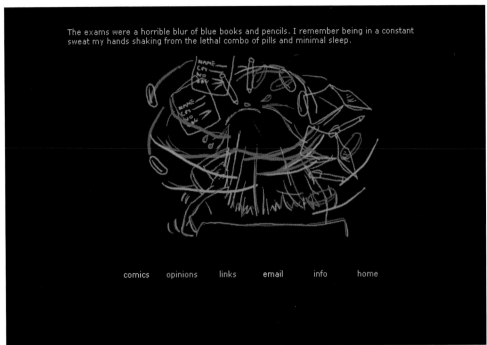

The exams were a horrible blur of blue books and pencils. I remember being in a constant sweat my hands shaking from the lethal combo of pills and minimal sleep.

comics   opinions   links   email   info   home

'Most of *Traced*'s audience did not read comics before and are not even webcomic readers. My work is syndicated to a couple of sites for teens and women, so it's part of a larger pool of content. People come to my stories because they like the content, not because they care that they are digital comics. I also get a lot of viewers who are interested in a specific storyline. When I put up the getting drunk comic, for a month a website dedicated to celebrating drunkenness linked to me. This is why the Web is so powerful – people come to your work through search engines, through portals, through links people put in their online diaries. In a way, what's happening is we're getting a whole new audience that's not so involved in the question of comics, but are very much interested in good stories.'

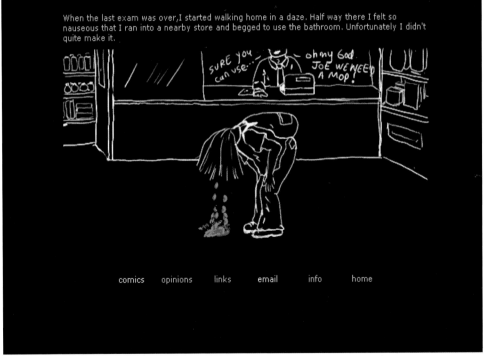

When the last exam was over, I started walking home in a daze. Half way there I felt so nauseous that I ran into a nearby store and begged to use the bathroom. Unfortunately I didn't quite make it.

SURE YOU can use...   oh my God. JOE WE NEED A MOP!

comics   opinions   links   email   info   home

Above and left: *Images from White's autobiographical comic,* Traced.

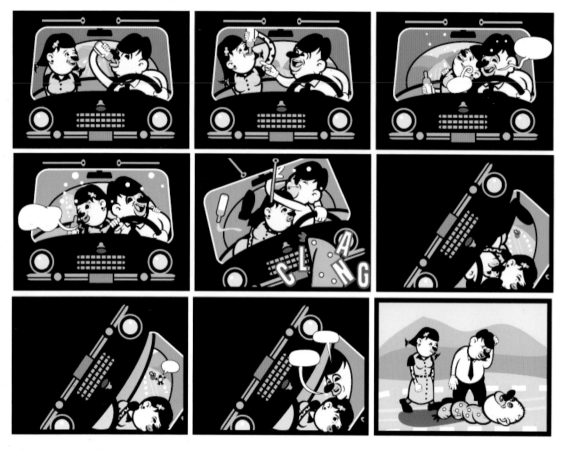

COUNTRY:
US

SITE ADDRESS:
WWW.EP.TC

HARDWARE:
MACINTOSH, SCANNER,
STAT CAMERA

SOFTWARE:
ADOBE PHOTOSHOP, ADOBE
ILLUSTRATOR

ethan persoff

Above: *Panel from Persoff's digital brain child,* Teddy.

> ❛ The computer helps complicated mechanical processes become less time-consuming. It's an amazing editor, too. The Web has brought a larger and more diverse audience to my work. Weblogs, link lists and e-mail bring an immediate response from readers, which is nice. ❜

'Here's where I probably disagree with most people who've put work online – especially the infinite canvas crowd and anything that requires a plug-in, or laborious scrolling down and over through the screen. I think for comics to work online, they need to just be comics and focus on storytelling. One thing that seems interesting about the Internet is that, beyond the occasional obnoxious bell and whistle, it's largely a series of still images with words, one image (or website) at a time. Comics seem to be perfect for exploiting that. For comics to move forwards online, cartoonists need to focus on what makes comics work – pacing, dialogue, lettering, panel juxtapositions and so on. This is extremely important because the Internet allows no limits on colour or page count, so, really, learning to be your own editor and set limits on yourself seems crucial. Otherwise, webcomics seem sloppy and self-indulgent.'

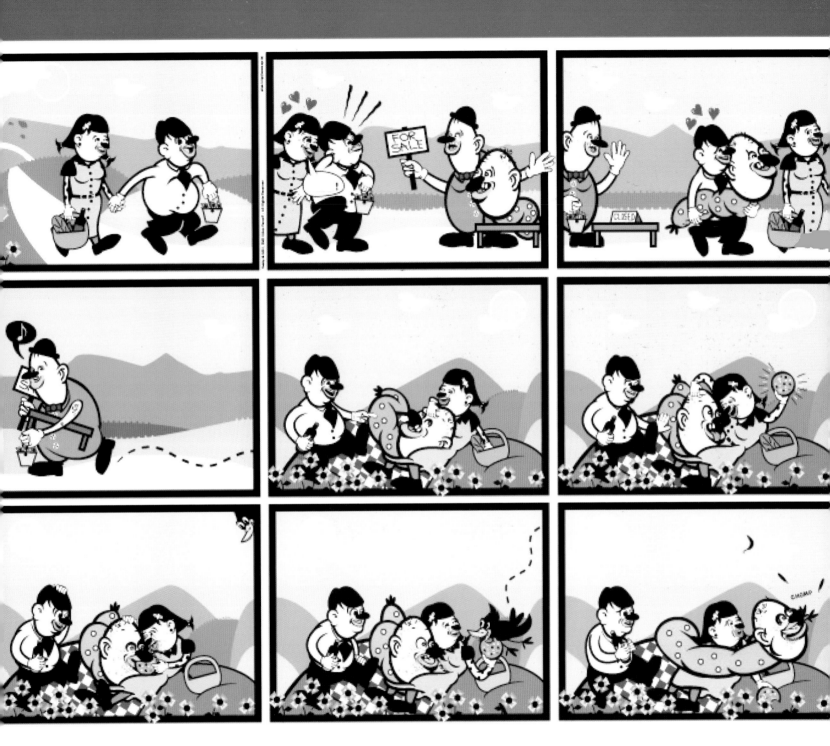

CHAPTER SIX

A SHOWCASE OF THE MOST EXCITING COMPOSITIONS IN THE BUSINESS

toon symphonies

Whether silent or soundtracked, cartoons have an inherent musical quality. Master cartoonists invest their drawings with melody and rhythm, time and timbre, harmony and rhyme.

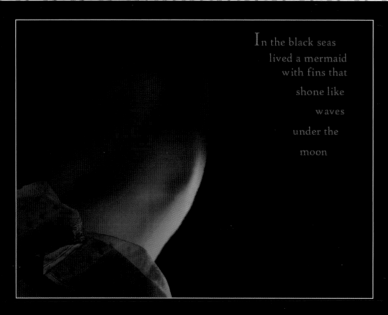

'I work by slowly coaxing an idea from scattered pieces into a whole reality. I often immediately have a sense of what the finished product should feel like, but it is often very vague and general. Most of my art process involves thinking about why the logic of the situation demands that the art be done in one style or another. I write many notes, make many quick sketches.

'My goal is storytelling that combines beautiful art with a thoughtful and compelling story, told through a method which surprises, shocks, or intrigues. And that desire to embrace anything except the traditional is what makes, and will make, my work stand out.'

Rigel Stuhmiller

Left and right: *Rigel Stuhmiller posts her work, including her intimate retelling of* The Little Mermaid *(left page) using Photoshop and Flash, at www.drenculture.com.*

COUNTRY:
US

SITE ADDRESS:
WWW.DAVIDGADDIS.COM

HARDWARE:
POWERMAC G3, SCANNER, WACOM
GRAPHICS TABLET

SOFTWARE:
ADOBE PHOTOSHOP, ADOBE
ILLUSTRATOR

david gaddis

'I never really had a sense of colour until I started working in Photoshop and Illustrator and was able to experiment with multiple colour combinations, undo previous choices and see the effects of adding or subtracting certain amounts of colour from the entire composition. I probably could have picked up the same things with painting, but not with such a rapid learning curve, and I probably wouldn't have been inclined to experiment with colour in comics at all without the computer. Also, I don't think I would have been inclined to experiment with a painterly look in comics without the computer, since photo reproduction of traditional painting is always so far off from the original it makes me want to cry. The conventional wisdom in the illustration and cartooning community is that an artist has to be thoroughly trained in traditional media in order to do solid work with a computer; while I don't think I could have learned to draw with a computer, my experience with colour runs completely counter to that.'

'A handful of people, like Tristan Farnon and Patrick Farley, are doing comics for the Internet that take advantage of its unique aesthetic properties, and many, many more are doing work that's obviously intended to appear in print somewhere down the road. Most cartoonists want to be in print, and this is quite reasonable; books and magazines are still superior reading devices to computer screens, the reading public shows no sign of giving them up, and new technologies show no sign of improving on them. We have yet to see whether the public will accept digital paper as a replacement, whenever that comes along, but at any rate it adopts the same format – an admission of its basic utility.

'I wish more people were doing Internet-only comics, because the aesthetic success of comics, wherever they appear, depends in large part on the extent to which the creator responds to and takes advantage of the format. But I think the reason we're not seeing that is that the debate surrounding online comics has treated the issue as if it's a matter of working entirely online versus working entirely in print, and not a lot of people are interested in working entirely online. What everyone seems to forget is that the Internet doesn't come with an exclusivity contract. Making comics for the Internet is a great way to drum up interest for your work, even if your main interest is print. Comics designed for the screen are far more compelling and persuasive for that purpose than black-and-white scans of your great American graphic novel.'

Above: *Pages from Gaddis's wordless but intimately expressive short story,* Piercing.

woodrow phoenix

'When designing for print, you often can't tell whether much of your content works as intended until you see the final thing printed – by which time, of course, it's too late to change it. Initially, I used the computer as a proofing tool. Once I got past trying to accurately predict my final artefact, I began using it more like a tool-box. I can easily combine typographical and pictorial elements, try endless variations in colour, texture and placement; all the elements of a design remain fluid till the last possible moment, so the stress of working in traditional media, where you can't afford to make a mistake, is removed. That's the crucial thing: freedom to experiment. Now that we have the Web, nothing need ever be finished, just iterated. I'm still undecided about whether this fosters true creativity or finicky neurosis.'

A selection of Phoenix's images, including a page from Pants Ant (above right), which will be screened as a cartoon on Cartoon Network in August 2003, and a series of stills from an online animation, Net Worth (right).

COUNTRY:

UK

SITE ADDRESSES:

WWW.SLAVELABOR.COM

WWW.CARNEY-PHOENIX.COM

WWW.COMICCOMPANY.COM

WWW.IQUITONLINE.COM

HARDWARE:

MACINTOSH G4, UMAX II A3
SCANNER

SOFTWARE:

ADOBE PHOTOSHOP, ADOBE
ILLUSTRATOR, MACROMEDIA
FONTOGRAPHER, ADOBE
STREAMLINE

COUNTRY:
US

SITE ADDRESSES:
WWW.MODERNTALES.COM
WWW.WHIMVILLE.COM
WWW.MAGICINKWELL.COM

HARDWARE:
MACINTOSH G3

SOFTWARE:
ADOBE PHOTOSHOP, MACROMEDIA
FREEHAND, ADOBE STREAMLINE

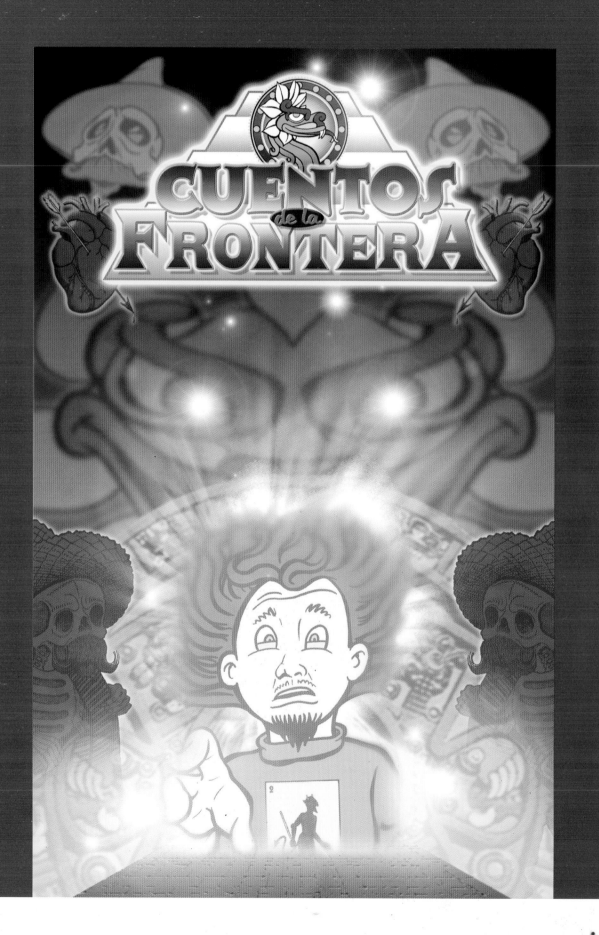

cayetano 'cat' garza jr

' *I've been quite fortunate in that I'm one of a handful of people who started to play around with the new medium early on in the game and have subsequently been touted (by others) as one of its innovators.* '

'I'm able to produce "panels" and images virtually anywhere with any type of materials I want. With the computer, suddenly all the restrictions that used to limit the production of comic art have been taken away. We're able to "fix" anything with the computer.'

149

scott christian sava

' *I think the greatest challenge for digital cartoonists in the near future will be the creative process. Once the tools get good enough, there are no more excuses. Now we have to develop a look that is not trying to mimic reality...or cartoons. We should develop a look that is natural to CGI, and push that as a medium.* '

Above: *Cavorting characters from Sava's creator-owned 3D print comic,* The Lab, *published by Astonish Comics.*

Sava, who has extensive experience in both comics and animation, was also the artist behind Spider-Man: Quality of Life, *published in 2002 by Marvel Comics.*

ESTEBAN

LIVINGSTON

COUNTRY:
US

SITE ADDRESSES:
WWW.BLUEDREAMSTUDIOS.COM

HARDWARE:
BOXX WORKSTATION,
DUAL 2.2 GHZ XEONS

SOFTWARE:
3D STUDIO MAX,
ADOBE PHOTOSHOP

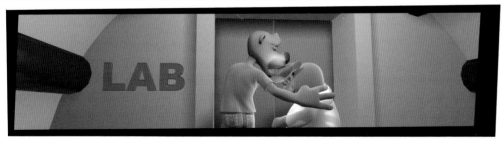

'No matter what tools you use, you have to be a good storyteller in comics. So my first task was to do layouts of each page. I did sketches in my sketchbook and thumbnailed out the whole issue. Then I'd scan the pages in and do colour designs for the pages. This helped me get an overall mood and feel for each scene. Then, from there, I would load up the environments and then the characters and pose them to give them the look I wanted for each frame. I would then tweak the lights to get the right effect and then render the frame out. Do this five to seven times, and you have your page.'

'Removing the compositional structure of pages has been interesting. Now I can just draw on any old piece of paper I have around, scan it and add it to my story. New possibilities of repetition and spacing.

Colour has been an exciting addition, too. I haven't even bothered moving beyond a Web-safe palette and have had such fun adding colour, trying to make it striking and pleasing.'

jason turner

'I come from a zine background, and my Web work has been a fairly direct extension of that. The immediacy of doing a zine comic and printing it right away is furthered so that I don't even have to go to a copy shop to "publish" my stuff. And it is immediately accessible to my readers. This can be a curse and a blessing, because readers want instant and constant gratification. So if a week goes by without updates, they get ornery. This does compel me to draw more, but I seem to feel more guilty when I don't.'

Tuesday was my Day Off.

Breakfast leaned towards the inedible.

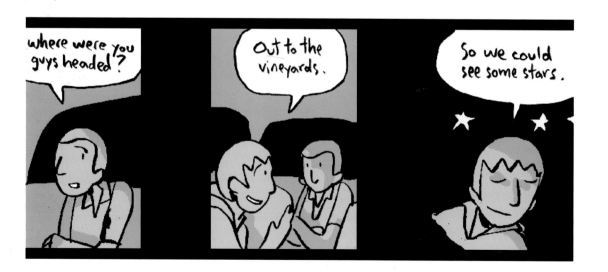

COUNTRY:

CANADA

SITE ADDRESSES:

WWW.STRONGMANPRESS.COM

HARDWARE:

PENTIUM PC, SCANNER

SOFTWARE:

ADOBE PHOTOSHOP,
MACROMEDIA HOMESITE

And this is where
my Stupid Week
really began.

A course for
work on my
day off?!!

Above: *Turner's wide
assortment of work,
including his weekly
True Loves, is a potent
mixture of invention and
improvisation.*

john barber

'I never really thought of myself as somebody who'd even HAVE a computer until 1998 or so. I did graphic design for the university newspaper at UC San Diego, so I sort of knew how to do some stuff, but I didn't really think about using it for comics that much.

'Once I got a computer, I started playing around with drawing and thought it was a really good tool. Nowadays, I mostly use a combination of analogue and digital.

Photoshop really gives you a great deal of control over your images – from the actual creation to making sure it'll print or display right.

'And I'd literally never seen a Web page until around 1996. I wasn't interested in it, even after that – until I read Scott McCloud's *Reinventing Comics* and realized there might be something worthwhile here. So I learned how to design Web pages, learned Flash and became the worldwide rock-star cartoonist I am today.'

'I'm amazed that not many other people are using Flash to display their comics. The program works like it was written for it.'

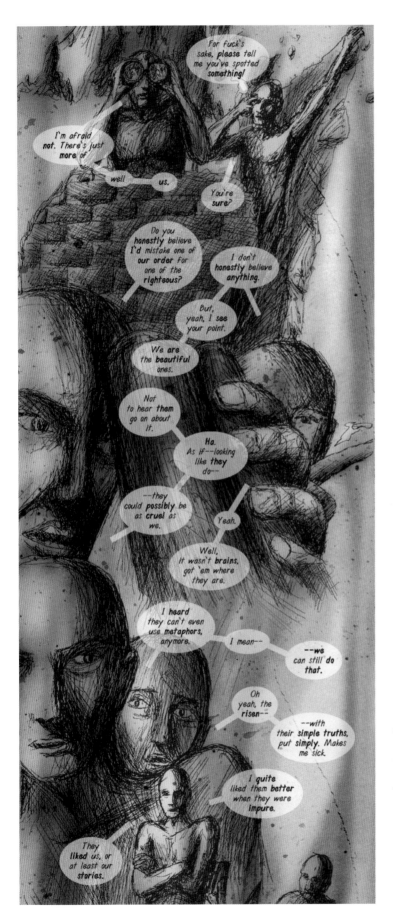

COUNTRY:

UK

SITE ADDRESSES:

WWW.MODERNTALES.COM

WWW.JOHNBARBERCOMICS.COM

HARDWARE:

SONY VAIO LAPTOP, WACOM
TABLET, AND CANON SCANNER

SOFTWARE:

ADOBE PHOTOSHOP, MACROMEDIA
FLASH, MACROMEDIA FREEHAND,
MACROMEDIA FONTOGRAPHER

' *My stuff isn't really experimental per se, and I try to be a formalist only in the sense that the form should enhance the reading experience. But this is a new medium, and I try not to bring all of my print baggage with me.* '

COUNTRY:
US

SITE ADDRESSES:
WWW.SULFURSTAR.COM
WWW.MODERNTALES.COM
WWW.TOPSHELFCOMIX.COM/
TOPSHELF/COMICS/SMITH/
BLACKMAGIC/INDEX.SHTML
HTTP://RICK_SMITH.HOME.
MINDSPRING.COM/COMICS/
MOROCCO/

HARDWARE:
WINDOWS 98 RUNNING ON A
PENTIUM 3 DELL TOWER, UMAX
ASTRA 1200S SCANNER

SOFTWARE:
ADOBE PHOTOSHOP, HIGH-LOGIC
FONT CREATOR, MACROMEDIA
FLASH

rick smith & tania menesse

‘ *The computer speeds up my creative process. I'm able to finish pages more quickly by colouring and lettering the comics (in my own handwriting) in Adobe Photoshop. The computer also enables me to electronically archive my work, making it safer from the ravages of time.* ’
Rick Smith

Left and right:
Smith and Menesse use a mood-altering, monochromatic palette in their genre-defying series, Shuck Comics.

> *'I first started using the computer just to colour my comics, but it was difficult to do something beyond that with just a mouse. But since I bought my Wacom tablet, I no longer use pencils, brushes or paper. From the first sketch to the final image, everything is done on the computer.'*

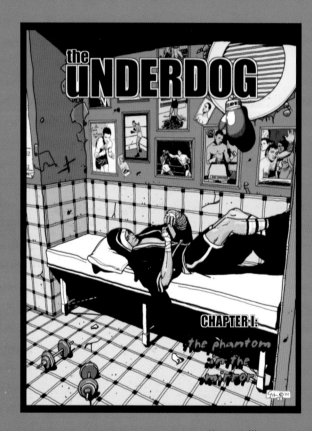

Above: *Unlike many 3D artists, Agudín uses CG modelling techniques to achieve an illustrative, rather than photorealistic, style in his digital comic,* The Underdog.

'I think it's important that the future artists, born in this new Internet era, don't ever forget how important it is to learn to draw the traditional way.

'With the computer, we have a new tool, but we still have to study, to learn about human anatomy, perspective, colour theory, lighting and shadows. Digital tools are great, and we are about to see a real boom in comics and animations with their help. But it can also be a real danger if artists forget their basis and start thinking that computers will draw for them.'

gil agudín

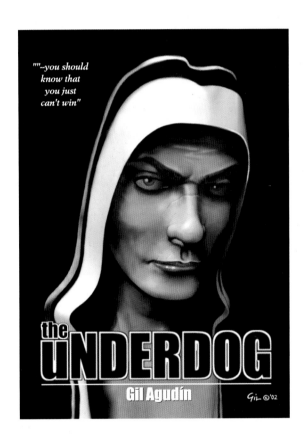

COUNTRY:
MEXICO

SITE ADDRESSES:
HTTP://UNDERDOG.DREAMCOMICS.COM

HARDWARE:
PENTIUM III, WACOM INTUOS2 TABLET

SOFTWARE:
COREL PHOTOPAINT 8, ADOBE PHOTOSHOP,
3D STUDIO MAX 2, CHARACTER STUDIO,
CARTOON REYES, ADOBE ILLUSTRATOR,
POSER 4, ACDSEE 2.22

anzovin studio

'Raf Anzovin's two independent short cartoons, *Java Noir* and *Puppet*, won nine international animation awards and were screened at Ottawa, IAF, VEAF, WAC, SIGGRAPH, NYAF, CalSUN, Anima Mundi, Imagina, Northampton FF, Melbourne IAF and other fests. Both cartoons star Dennis the Dog, a character Raf has been developing since childhood.

'As an animator, Raf specializes in fight animation and animating to music, character rigging and techniques of non-linear animation.

'We at Anzovin Studio prefer to stay small for now and leave as much time as possible for Raf's independent projects. We also spend quite a bit of time developing training materials to help novice animators, so you might say one of our important roles is as educators. Another is to bring high-end capabilities to non-technical artists; that's why we created The Setup Machine, a program that helps animators quickly create character rigs.'
Steve Anzovin

Above and right: *Images created by Raf and Steve Anzovin's father-and-son studio, which employs six artist/animators working mainly on games and commercials.*

COUNTRY:
US

SITE ADDRESSES:
WWW.ANZOVIN.COM

HARDWARE:
PC

SOFTWARE:
MAYA, LIGHTWAVE,
ANIMATION:MASTER,
CUSTOM SOFTWARE

' We strive to make 3D characters that are truly lively and expressive, that don't have the "animated corpse" look of so many CG creations. If anything, it's the "aliveness" of our characters that stands out. '

1994 (Age 12)	1996 (Age 14)	1998 (Age 16)	2000 (Age 18)	2002 (Age 20)
Stratavision 3D	Infini-D 4.0	Lightwave 5.0 for Mac	Animation:Master 8.5	Lightwave 7.5

...This gently interactive fairytale adventure will give you...

Nev...   Jagor

...a breath of the past, a breath of magic and the magic of past events.....

"Croatian Tales of Long Ago"
written in 1916 by
Ivana Brlic Mazuranic
www.bulaja.com/FAIRYTALES/
created by

Nathan Jurevicius / Laurence Arcadias / Al Keddie / Helena Bulaja

Edgar Beals / Katrin Rothe / Mirek Nisenbaum / Ellen McAuslan

DIRECTORS/ANIMATORS/CO-PRODUCERS:
HELENA BULAJA – CROATIA
LAURENCE ARCADIAS – FRANCE (NOW US)
ELLEN MCAUSLAN – UK
KATRIN ROTHE – GERMANY
NATHAN JUREVICIUS – AUSTRALIA
AL KEDDIE – UK
MIREK NISENBAUM – BELARUS (NOW US)
EDGAR BEALS – CANADA

SITE ADDRESSES:
WWW.BULAJA.COM/FAIRYTALES/

HARDWARE:
PC AND MAC

SOFTWARE:
MACROMEDIA FLASH, FREEHAND, ADOBE
PHOTOSHOP, ADOBE ILLUSTRATOR, COREL
DRAW

Above: *Introductory pages from the award-winning international collaboration,* Croatian Tales of Long Ago.

croatian tales of long ago

'As owner of Bujala Publishing, a multimedia publishing company that publishes books on CD-ROM, I started this project where I wanted to make real multimedia work inspired by one of Croatia's best fairytale books, written in 1916 by Brlic Mazuranic. My idea was to make a CD-ROM with eight stories as animated/interactive stand-alone pieces, each with a different team from a different part of the world. And thanks to digital technology, especially the Internet, I have found seven international teams to work with me, and I decided to make one story of my own. The *Croatian Tales* project will be published in October 2002 in three languages: Croatian, English and German.'

Helen Bulaja

Above: *Stills from the eight animated stories, each by a different team and depicting a different tale.*

'Croatia has a great animation tradition. Zagreb animation school was very popular in the world some 30 years ago, and in 1962, one of Croatia's best animators, D Vukotic, won an Oscar for his animated movie, *Surogat*. This film changed the perception of 2D animation at the time, but now Croatia's role in animation is very poor. Animators are not well connected with new digital tools, and there is no serious digital production here. This project, *Croatian Tales of Long Ago*, is the only serious digital animated project in Croatia, and many major critics and media people share the opinion that this is the best thing that has happened in Croatian cinematography in the last 10 years. This poor situation here, with animators who don't know how to use computers, pushed me to find people from other parts of the world to make this project.'
Helena Bulaja

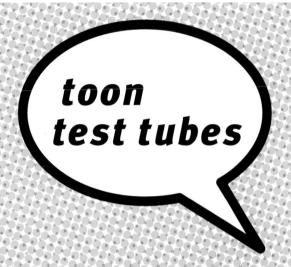

toon test tubes

Is the digital frontier as open and endless as some soothsayers have predicted? Ask these artists, who are determined to challenge cartooning's tried-and-tested rules and seek out new routes.

Throughout its history, cartooning has had more than its share of revolutionaries. McCay, Herriman, Disney, Eisner, Tezuka, Crumb, Moebius, Bakshi, Spiegelman – names that have come to signify radical change. The now familiar media of print and film were once just grand experiments. And the turn of the twenty-first century brings yet another. The pervasion of digital tools in the past few decades has incited a rash of new rebellions, the outcomes of which are still anyone's guess. The potential of digital production and delivery is staggering, and yet, with the recent influx to the Web of the most diverse group of cartoonists the world has ever seen, the cultural rebellions that have accompanied such technological innovation may prove to be even more far-reaching. This showcase has given only a tiny glimpse of the mass of voices and visions that can be heard and seen online, on film and in print thanks to digital technology.

Below and right: Images from Mark Martin's collection of oddities, www.markmartin.net, which the artist says is 'constantly mutating'.

'What will the future bring for digital cartoons? Cranial implants. You may be able to plug in and take a psychedelic trip. The porno industry may HYPER-explode, exponentially more than it recently has due to the Internet alone. The possibilities for pumped-in experience may be limitless! As this Revolution of the Mind unfurls, I may still be drawing cartoons in linear panels. There may still be people who appreciate the "quaintness".'

Mark Martin

scott mccloud

'Lately, there's been a growing concern (sometimes with Yours Truly as a prime target) that the comics world – both online and print – is being overrun with empty experiments; that comics artists have somehow forgotten how to tell good stories, and are content to just play with form and offer nothing of any lasting human value or interest. Like most such collective observations, this one is at least half-right. Since the mid-90s, interest in comics as a form definitely hit a new high and a lot of the small press scene took a distinct turn for the experimental, with a highly experimental wing of online creators not far behind.

'The "all-form-no-content" complaint tends to overlook the historic function of such periods, however. Hardly any of the aggressively experimental creators working in the last 10 years were really turning their back on storytelling for good.

COUNTRY:
US

SITE ADDRESSES:
WWW.SCOTTMCCLOUD.COM

HARDWARE:
POWER MAC G4, WACOM INTUOS TABLET

SOFTWARE:
ADOBE PHOTOSHOP, ADOBE ILLUSTRATOR, ADOBE GOLIVE, BBEDIT LITE, FETCH, MACROMEDIA FLASH

Many of those art-school refugees sporting day-glo silk-screened minis at Small Press Expo are hard at work today on their own graphic novels and have plenty of stories to tell us, and, if history is any indication, will be all the better as storytellers having taken those experimental roads early on. And though formal experimentation is still important for the webcomics scene to find its shape in the next few years, there's also a growing body of great storytelling online that's bound to grow in quantity and quality throughout this decade.'

Left: *A 'long shot' of McCloud's* Zot! Online: Hearts and Minds *(2000) showing an early incarnation of the 'infinite canvas' format where each column represents a chapter and the computer monitor is used as a 'window' for reading comics.*

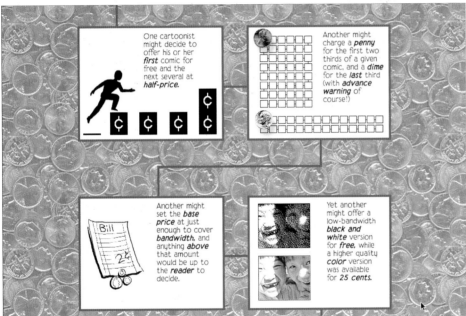

Above left and right: *Examples of McCloud's wide array of webcomics. The above images from* Zot! Online: Hearts and Minds *and* I Can't Stop Thinking #6: Coins of the Realm *(an essay in which McCloud discusses the benefits of a* micropayment system for webcomics) *use linking lines called 'trails' between panels that, McCloud argues, offer numerous storytelling advantages including distance pacing (where 'to move in space is to move in time'), narrative* subdivision, sustained rhythm and gradualism. The Parallelogram's Revenge *(right), which McCloud calls 'a geometric Rorschach test', is from the experimental and audience-interactive* Morning Improv *series.*

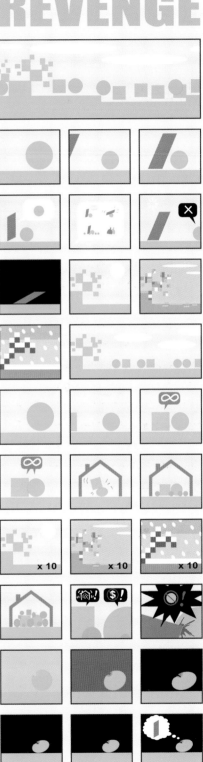

xdude

' *Awkward frame-by-frame drawing has definitely had its day. While the conceptual sketch will never cease to exist, I think movie houses have definitely seen the benefit of making computers do the "tweening" work. If you can get smoother, higher-quality animation produced at a fraction of the cost, why do it any other way? Will 2D animation continue to exist? For at least 10 years, I believe so. There is something charismatic about simple 2D cartoon characters.* '

the digital dude presents

"the dough"
a special animated feature

based on a true story

'As a child, I was always captivated whenever I saw moving images on a computer, but good animation programs just didn't exist at the time (unless you liked typing hundreds of lines of code). The first time I made a little red circle move across the screen in Flash 3, it was as if my childhood dream had been fulfilled. Since then, I've learned through trial and error – the walking animation of the man in *The Dough* alone took me three days to complete. My works have won a number of awards, including the Shocked Site of the Day, Cool Site of the Day and the 1999 International Internet Film Festival award for Best Sound.'

'Communication is really the key. Holding someone's attention on the Internet for 30 seconds is a huge accomplishment; telling a four-minute-long story like *The Dough* requires a lot of pace changes, music changes and visual theme changes. Effective use of sound is also required; sound is fully half the experience. On a medium such as the Internet, the almighty file size dictates which pieces will be successful and which ones won't.'

Above and right: *The enigmatic XDude's Flash film,* The Dough, *combines text, moving image and soundtrack in one brief but brilliant sequence.*

COUNTRY:
CANADA

SITE ADDRESSES:
WWW.XDUDE.COM

SOFTWARE:
MACROMEDIA FLASH, GOLDWAVE
(SOUND EDITING)

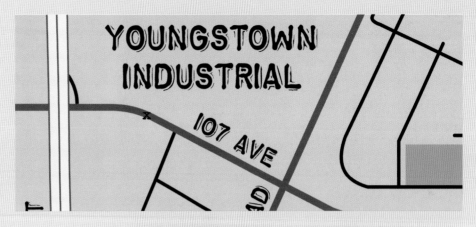

Next time it happens,
don't get mad.

Get even.

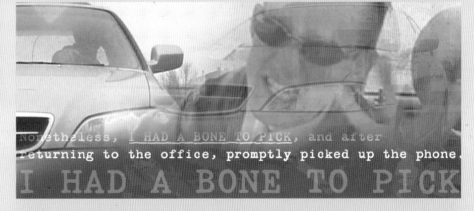

Nonetheless, I HAD A BONE TO PICK, and after
returning to the office, promptly picked up the phone.

I HAD A BONE TO PICK

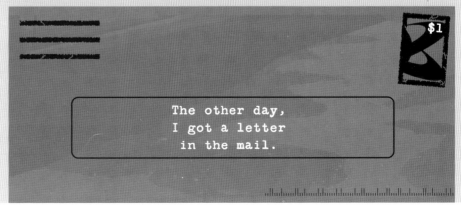

The other day,
I got a letter
in the mail.

169

Right: *Images from* Delta Thrives *(top)*, Barracuda: The Scotty Zaccharine Story *(middle) and* The Spiders *(bottom)*.

patrick farley

COUNTRY:
US

SITE ADDRESSES:
WWW.E-SHEEP.COM

HARDWARE:
MACINTOSH

SOFTWARE:
ADOBE PHOTOSHOP, ADOBE
ILLUSTRATOR, CURIOUS LABS
POSER, COREL BRYCE,
MACROMEDIA FLASH

'*Patrick Farley's long-running* E-Sheep *contains some of the best writing in comics today. Wherever you think he's going by panel 10, he'll always surprise you by panel 100. Farley's comics also explore a wide variety of art styles, from the kaleidoscopic collages of* Chrysalis Colossus, *to the lush 3D of* Shapeshifter, *to the Flash delerium of* Apocamon.'

Scott McCloud

'*The tools you use affect the story you tell. The important thing is not to let the tools dictate the way you tell that story.*'

Patrick Farley

Below: *A small segment of Farley's masterful science-fiction webcomic,* Delta Thrives, *which uses the horizontal scrolling format to superb effect.*

COUNTRY:
CANADA

SITE ADDRESSES:
WWW.BEETLEBLUE.COM
WWW.MEOMI.COM
WWW.NDROID.COM

HARDWARE:
APPLE POWERBOOK G4, AGFA
SCANNER

SOFTWARE:
ADOBE PHOTOSHOP, ADOBE
ILLUSTRATOR, MACROMEDIA
FLASH, MACPAINT, INFINI-D

vicki wong

'I think first it is important to distinguish between a digital comic and a digital animation. What is the difference? If we have limited animation in a panel comic, does it become an animation? And if we add interactivity to it, does it just become a game? Is the video game (with the animation and the interactivity, so to speak) the final frontier where everything else is heading?

'I have a love/hate relationship with my computer. But I tend to be very fond of many visual styles that only the computer can create well (such as pixel detailing). The greatest thing about creating on the computer is the potential to programme interactivity into imagery – interactivity beyond page flipping.

'The reason why the Web is great for artistic expression is that it provides the artist with immediate access to his or her audience (and the audience to the artist). Creation can become much more of a dialogue. Whether the audience actually influences what the artist creates, or simply just having your audience directly respond to you – personally and emotionally – it is both inspiring and gratifying.'

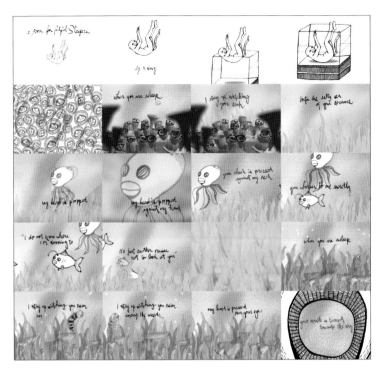

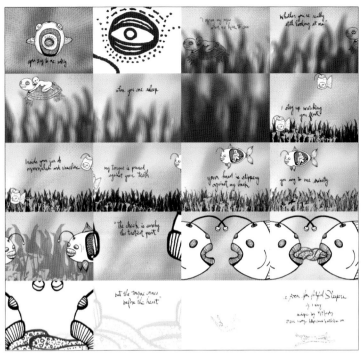

> ' I create in a wide variety of media and formats, depending on what the goal is. In general I tend to prefer either single-panel "visual poems" or interactive animations, usually involving critters. But mainly monkeys, often in strange emotional states. '

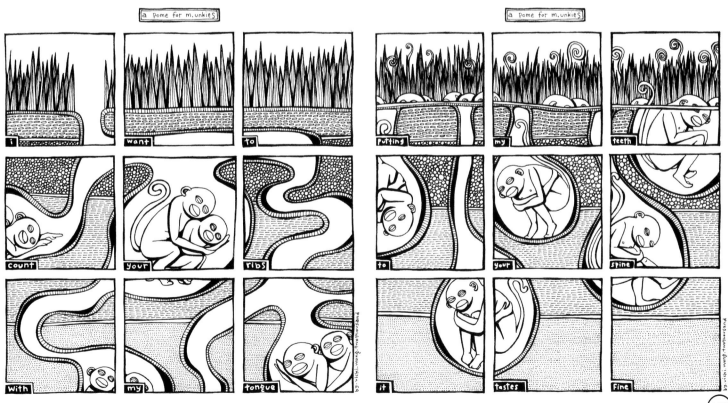

'*What makes my work stand out from the crowd? The fact that I'm not only experimenting, but that I'm also following the few rules of timing, rhythm and simplicity of information that every picture contains. At the same time, I'm always aware that I'm working for an audience, not only for myself.*'

demian.5

'Computers gave me lots of excitement for being creative. As the first "powerful" Apples arrived in my workplace around 1994, they hooked me. They gave me so many things to do and try, nearly unlimited artistic possibilities. I've always been drawing comics in the "normal" way, but I never had the patience to really finish some longer work. Always erasing, correcting, drawing again was quite unnerving. Drawing with the computer ended that problem. I found a way to create "multifunctional" characters and landscapes in Adobe Illustrator. It became very easy then not only to correct and perfect the drawings but also, by simply copying and changing the characters' movements, I think I became faster in the work's progress. The Web also added much to my motivation to continue drawing comics. It gave me the possibility to show my first serious work to an audience around the world, which gave me some direct feedback in turn. The Web also gave me unlimited artistic freedom and independence. No one ever told me what to do. There are no publishers, no editors, no directors, no clients giving you corrections of details you never would correct yourself. I just love it.

'Digital comics already are the ideal platform for every independent comics artist. The new underground is changing media. The Web becomes richer and richer, every hour, every day.'

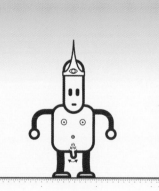
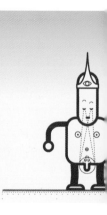

COUNTRY:
SWITZERLAND

SITE ADDRESSES:
WWW.DEMIAN5.COM

HARDWARE:
MACINTOSH G4

SOFTWARE:
ADOBE ILLUSTRATOR, ADOBE
PHOTOSHOP, ADOBE IMAGEREADY,
MAXON CINEMA 4D XL, MACROMEDIA
DREAMWEAVER

Below, and left: *Pages
from* When I Am King, *
showing the artist's
unique choice of formats.*

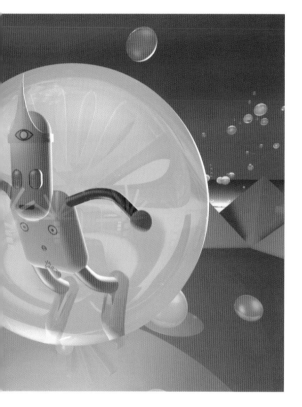

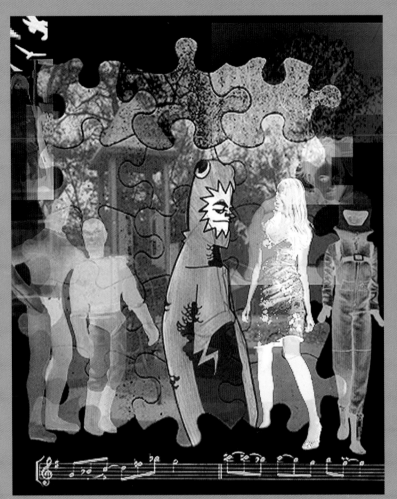

' *The Internet is a very open and limitless medium. I can get colour that couldn't be achieved in print. I can get a level of texture that would be lost on paper. I'm not bound to a paper size or page number. It's so open-ended. But it's not permanent. A book is permanent. A webseries can be erased in a few minutes. It's kind of nerve-racking, but it's good practice.* '

Above left and right:
Images from Lex's 'raw and expressionistic' The Aweful Science Fair *and* Lunar Cadaver.

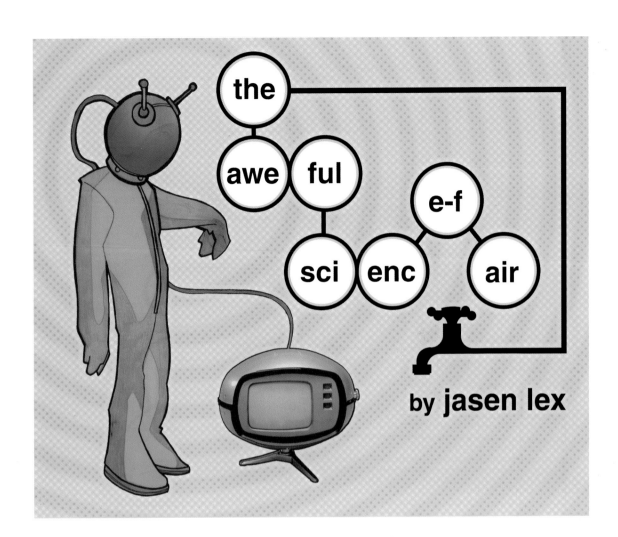

the aweful e-f scienc air

by jasen lex

COUNTRY:
US

SITE ADDRESSES:
WWW.OPI8.COM
WWW.LEXOTRONIC.8M.COM
WWW.MODERNTALES.COM

HARDWARE:
'AN AGEING MACINTOSH, A
SCANNER AND SOME DIFFERENT
CAMERAS.'

SOFTWARE:
ADOBE PHOTOSHOP

jasen lex

'My work wouldn't be completed if I didn't have a computer. It allows me to develop material and find colours and mix stuff together so fast that there is no other way to achieve that kind of quality of art. I was extremely sloppy as a fine artist, and this is the only way I can do that stuff neatly and quickly.

'The Web has been such a great aid in the whole process because there's that instant feedback. You can release a comic on the Web, and a few hours later people write and tell you what they think. And doing that in a monthly schedule just forces you to become a better storyteller, or at least pushes you to think further. And if people tell you you stink, it makes you want to try harder to shut them up.'

FASTER?

FASTER!

HOLD TIGHT.

FLYING FYN TAXIS

YAAAAAAHOOOOOOOOO!!!

TSK. HUMANS!

TAXI

THE NIGHT BEFORE   SIXGUN

COUNTRY:
UK

SITE ADDRESSES:
WWW.E-MERL.COM

HARDWARE:
PC, DIGITAL CAMERA, SCANNER

SOFTWARE:
MACROMEDIA FLASH, ADOBE
PHOTOSHOP, JASC PAINTSHOP
PRO, POSER 4, MACROMEDIA
DREAMWEAVER, SOUNDFORGE

daniel merlin goodbrey

'I think I'm still one of the few people really trying to push the hypercomic format to see what it can do. Webcomics are beginning to settle down a bit as a medium, but the possibilities of hypercomics are still wide open. It's a medium that needs more creators willing to try out every different crazy idea they can, so that we can find out what works and what doesn't.

'One thing [that] working with a computer offers is fluidity. Rather than having distinct stages of production from script through to finished artwork, I tend to jump around a lot from one area of the creative process to another. This process could quickly lead to disaster if I were working with traditional tools, but with new media I've found it can lead to a much stronger finished product (especially where hyperfiction is concerned). For example, working on screen means I can easily adapt my ideas as I progress, testing out different elements of composition and navigation before selecting the best fit for the story.'

Above: *Still from Goodbrey's highly acclaimed* Sixgun: Tales of An Unfolded Earth.

Right: *Disparate images from two of Goodbrey's 'new experiments in fiction',* Sixgun *and* Doodleflak.

‘ *Taking a medium that's built for the printed page and mutating it into something at home on the ever-changing canvas of the World Wide Web...that's the real challenge of creating digital comics.* ’

tristan farnon

' *Tristan Farnon's* Leisuretown.com *is a thermonuclear spitball; a massive collection of photo-comics starring an assortment of poseable plastic (rubber?) animals, careering from one nihilistic self-destructive episode to another. Don't miss the classics* Down By The Freeway, Rhapsody In Yellow *and* Nobody Came To My Winter Solstice Party. '

Scott McCloud

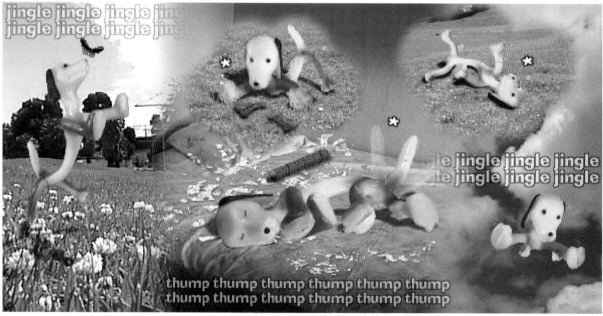

COUNTRY:
US

SITE ADDRESS:
WWW.LEISURETOWN.COM

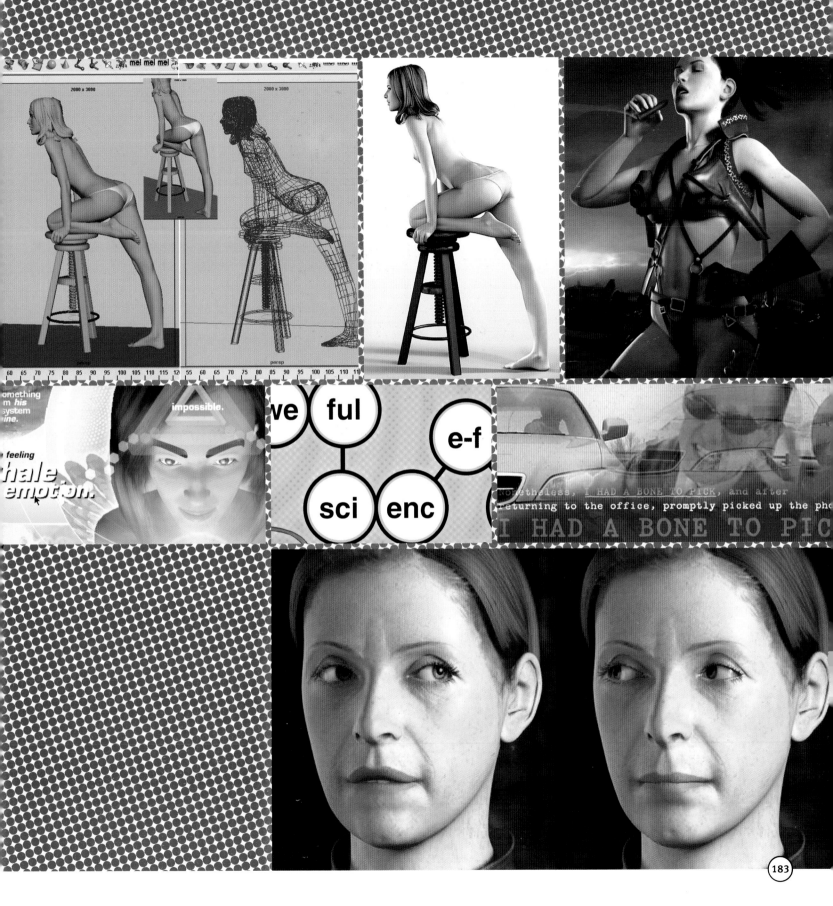

New routes, new risks

I asked the many cartoonists featured in this book for their thoughts on what challenges and opportunities the future might bring for digital cartoons. Here is a small selection of their answers.

Tracy A White

The future of digital comics is wide open and largely dependent on how cartoonists embrace technology and the evolution of audience/reader interaction that gaming has introduced into storylines. Most kids growing up (and quite a few adults, myself included) play some type of digital game that involves a narrative structure.

I'd like to think there would be room for collaborative narratives based on a single vision. Sort of the way *The Sims* game creates an environment in which you build the story based on choices you make. At the same time, I can't help but hold onto the idea that people will also continue to want comics with the beginning, middle and end worked out for them. Or perhaps there will be total immersion comics where a community of people (maybe friends?) tell a story together, and then other stories where the creator has most of the control, and still others where there is some sort of balance between the artist's vision and user input. I think it is going to depend a lot on what people think is good storytelling and what people want to get out of the experience. Once again, it comes down to experimentation, which is what we should be doing with such a young medium.

How comics get delivered to people will also change the way they are presented. Will the fan of the future receive comics over a video watch or an interactive rollable thin screen, or through some mechanism in a flashy pair of sunglasses? Or some other medium we can't even imagine today? As technology moves forwards, comics will change because each generation of artists will need to take into consideration the different parameters that a technological leap provides. 3D comics, comics with audio, comics that respond to voice input... it's all possible.

Gareth Hinds

At some point, we will have a real digital paper/e-book solution, and print periodicals will disappear. That means ongoing comic series will pretty much have to be digital delivery only. There will still be a place for graphic novels for a while after that, but someday paper books will be in the same collectors-only space as hand-typeset artist books are today, and the average joe will read everything on a holo-cube – or in the case of straight prose – have it read to him (already I know a lot of people who

consume more audiobooks than printed books). I can't quite picture what comics will be like then, but I'm sure they will explode into infinitely more variations of form than we have seen yet.

Jenni Gregory

I think the future for digital comics is very bright. I think that there will soon be a growing and thriving market for comic collections distributed on CD and DVD. I think that low-cost Internet subscription services will become both viable and popular as soon as broadband Internet service becomes the standard and bandwidth costs get in line with market forces and begin to drop. I think that once digital cartoonists begin to be compensated appropriately (and, if I may be allowed to dream, handsomely) for their work, then new entrants into the field will explode. Comics artists who are currently working only in print will begin to enter the digital market, bringing their hardcore, print-comics-only fans with them. And I hope that digital comics will be able to avoid the triple curse of print comics: (1) the over-domination of one genre (superheroes) to the point of exclusion of anything that dares to be different; (2) the stigma that says anyone over the age of fourteen reading a comic is either a geek or a simpleton; and (3) the 'boys-club'/'tree-fort' mentality that is pervasive in every facet of print comics, from creation to distribution to sales.

Charley Parker

In the near future, I think it will continue as it's going: a few hardy pioneers who are willing to put a lot of work into creative, original online comics, basically at their own expense, bracketed by hundreds of commercial and fan sites with little real content. Unfortunately, I think this will continue until there is some better mechanism for independent creators to actually make income from their work. A universal system of micropayments is often discussed as the holy grail in this respect, a system that would allow 'Click here to pay 50 cents to read this story', without the necessity of signing up or entering credit card information. Sadly, that option seems even more remote than it did a few years ago. In the long run, if those issues can be resolved, the potential is enormous. Digital comics could expand into a new realm of multilayered interactive storytelling, taking a place somewhere among traditional comics, film and games.

Christian Gossett

With comics in particular, it's basically acceptance of this new form with its very different looks and possibilities. Comics are almost like poetry in the way that there are many purists and fundamentalists who want the same old rhyme and verse, and the same methodologies. Innovation is always met with fierce resistance from those who prefer the complacency of the status quo, and digital artists with their love of new technology are fighting against a century of outmoded techniques and those that cling to yesterday's heroes, yesterday's forms of storytelling and yesterday's production processes. The thing is, we've seen how the future is inevitable, and as the old-timers say, 'Pioneers get all the arrows'. In the long term, time is on our side, and we will change the way graphic storytelling is done. It's already too late to put the genie back in the bottle. Elsewhere, as a digital illustrator, there are simply endless possibilities. From movie posters to character design, to modern commercial graphics, the only challenge is raising one's level of talent to a point where people want to start giving you money to do whatever it is you do.

Steve Anzovin

Within the animation industry, there's intense pressure to produce animated content as cheaply as possible. The trend, which you can see already, is strongly towards very stylised, low-cost 2D animation that is propelled mainly by bold visual style, engaging characters, snappy writing and distinctive vocal talent, not by naturalism or expressivity of motion. At the upper end, you'll see ever-more-elaborate and expensive 3D or hybrid 2D/3D features developed by a handful of brand-name studios (Pixar, PDI, Blue Sky, Dreamworks, Disney), but still propelled mainly by a bold visual style, engaging characters, snappy writing and distinctive vocal talent. The industry is in a downturn right now, reflecting the general economic slowdown. Studios with uncontrolled overheads are going under; many independent artists find it hard to make ends meet as competition gets fierce. On the other hand, animation continues to penetrate more areas of entertainment and communication. There are all kinds of new opportunities. One of Raf Anzovin's mentors runs a company that provides character-animated content for mobile phone displays.

Adapting comics from the Web to TV
by Tracy A White

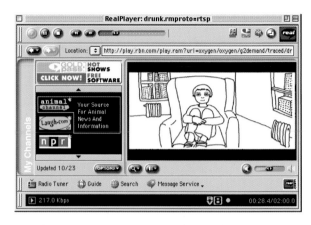

Two years ago, I developed *Traced* as an animated TV series for Oxygen Media, and those segments ended up back on the Web in a streamed format. The challenge was twofold: How do you take a static, silent webcomic and turn it into something dynamic enough for TV while trying to maintain some of Traced's webcomic roots? And, of course, tell the best possible story.

I didn't want the comic to look like traditional, fast-paced TV animation because it's not – it was originally a comic. Because I'm not an animator, I worked closely with an Avid editor, and since neither of us had much animation background, we were able to come up with interesting solutions to keep the pace moving without using fluid movements. First, we inversed the colours because all black did not look great on a TV monitor, and then we tried to create a sense of movement by adding a soundtrack to limited animations. I made the mouths of the characters move. Trust me, when you watch something on TV and hear a character speak, the mouth has to move or it just doesn't work. That, and the eyes need to blink. Over time, the TV shorts got better and better, and we were luckily able to experiment. From a storytelling angle, each episode needed to be three minutes long, so I was able to add details to the storyline that were not in the original Web-based version. Finally, the HTML-based text in the comic ended up being the text spoken by the narrator (me), who appears at the beginning of each episode.

When the comic was streamed on the Web, it actually benefited from the reason most TV shows don't look good streamed: the dropped frame. I'm not a streaming expert, but, as I understand it, during compression frames get dropped to make the whole file a little smaller, so if there's lots of movement, the nuances get lost. Since *Traced* didn't have lots of animation, the streams came out relatively clean.

Finally, the small animations that I started using for *Traced* on TV to bring out details, I've now incorporated into my webcomics.

A leap into the future

Above right Created and maintained by Rick Veitch and Steve Conley, COMICON.com is designed to be a '"virtual comics convention", where all participating cartoonists have an equal space, self-promotion is king and ideas are shared freely in a thriving online community. COMICON.com will surely be a model for future experiments in bringing digital cartoons to a mass audience worldwide.'

How do these visions of tomorrow catch your fancy?

    * Total sensory-immersion technology

    * Live animation with artificial intelligence

    * Real-time, interactive, multi-creator comics

    * 3-D animation tablets for toddlers

    * The Nobel Prize for Graphic Literature

    Even the most staunch preservationist among us – though I doubt such a person would read a book on digital cartooning – must admit there is some appeal to these ideas. And a few of them are actually in the works.

    Take a moment to throw aside your preconceptions of what is plausible or implausible, likely or unlikely, and let loose your imagination.

Now ask yourself, what subjects and images might be included in a book about digital cartooning just 10 years from now? How about 50 years from now? Would it even resemble a book? Will the concept of 'digital' be completely irrelevant by that time? And will the concepts of 'cartooning' and 'cartoonist' seem outdated? I sincerely hope not.

    If we fix our collective attention on cartooning's history, leaving ample room for unfettered speculation, then we will begin to shape the cartoons of the twenty-first century into an art form that is far-fetched, and yet familiar.

    Until then, let's keep drawing and see what happens.

toon reference guide

Below is a list of websites and books I recommend for your further investigation of digital cartooning. The list is far from comprehensive, but is a good start, nevertheless. Be sure also to visit the websites of the cartoonists featured in this book. You'll be glad you did.

Websites

Adventure Strips.com	http://www.adventurestrips.com
Animation World Network	http://www.awn.com
Anime Web Turnpike	http://www.anipike.com
Artbomb	http://www.artbomb.net
BDnet.com	http://www.bdnet.com
Bench Comics	http://www.benchcomics.com
CG-Char	http://www.cg-char.com
CBLDF	http://www.cbldf.org
Comic Book Resources	http://www.comicbookresources.com
COMICON.com	http://www.comicon.com
Digital Webbing	http://www.digitalwebbing.com
I Want My Flash TV!	http://www.iwantmyflashtv.com
Keenspot	http://www.keenspot.com
Komikwerks	http://www.komikwerks.com
Major 3D	http://www.major3D.com
Modern Tales	http://www.moderntales.com
NextComics	http://www.nextcomics.com
OPi8.com	http://www.opi8.com
Scott McCloud.com	http://www.scottmccloud.com
Sequential Tart	http://www.sequentialtart.com
Serializer.net	http://www.serializer.net
Talk About Comics.com	http://www.talkaboutcomics.com
The Comics Journal	http://www.tcj.com
3D-ARK	http://www.3dark.com
Wired.com	http://www.wired.com
Words and Pictures Museum	http://www.wordsandpictures.org
Zwol.org	http://www.zwol.org

Books

Animation, The Whole Story by Howard Beckerman (Amereon House, 2001)

Comics & Sequential Art by Will Eisner (Poorhouse Press, 1985)

Digital Character Animation by George Maestri (New Riders Publishing, 1996)

Flash Character Animation: Applied Studio Techniques by Lee Purcell (Sams Publishing, 2002)

Graphic Storytelling by Will Eisner (Poorhouse Press, 1996)

Manga! Manga! The World of Japanese Comics by Frederik L Schodt (Kodansha International, 1983)

Principles of Three-Dimensional Computer Animation by Michael O'Rourke (W.W. Norton & Company, 1998)

Reinventing Comics by Scott McCloud (HarperCollins, 2000)

Story: Substance, Structure, Style, and The Principles of Screenwriting by Robert McKee (HarperCollins, 1997)

The Animator's Workbook by Tony White (Watson-Guptill, 1988)

The Animator's Survival Kit by Richard Williams (Faber and Faber, 2001)

The History of Animation: Enchanted Drawings by Charles Solomon (Alfred A Knopf, 1989)

The Illusion of Life: Disney Animation by Frank Thomas and Ollie Johnston (Hyperion, 1995)

3D Creature Workshop by Bill Fleming (Charles River Media, 1998)

Understanding Comics: The Invisible Art by Scott McCloud (HarperCollins, 1993)

Acknowledgements

I'd like to extend my gratitude to all the creators who so generously shared their cartoons as well as their thoughts in the pages of this book.

My special thanks go to everyone at Ilex Press and Watson-Guptill, Alexander and Brandy Danner, Patrick Coyle, Shannon Denton, Scott McCloud, Jim Zubkavich, Roberto Corona, Bill Fleming, Steve and Raf Anzovin, Gene Deitch, Chris Bailey, Charley Parker, Charlie Athanas, Gary Chaloner, Will Eisner, Demian Vogler, Tracy A White, Brooke Burgess, Patrice Mailloux, Joe Zabel, Steven James Taylor and Gil Agudin.

This book would not have come to be without the loving support of my family and the graphic design expertise of my beautiful wife, Lesley, who deserves to be called co-author of this book.

Picture Acknowledgements

Index